ACTA UNIVERSITATIS UPSALIENSIS

Studia Doctrinae Christianae Upsaliensia

28

Anders Jeffner

Theology and Integration

Four Essays in Philosophical Theology

UPPSALA 1987
Distributed by:
Almqvist & Wiksell International
Stockholm – Sweden

Published with grants from The Swedish Council for Research in the Humanities and Social Sciences.

Abstract

Jeffner, A., 1987: Theology and Integration. Four Essays in Philosophical Theology. Acta Universitatis Upsaliensis. *Studia Doctrinae Christianae Upsaliensia* 28. 73 pp. Uppsala. ISBN 91-554-2087-7.

This book consists of four essays which deal with the relationship between religious truth-claims and non-religious knowledge. The first deals with historical examples of attempts to create an artificial world-language which can express an integrated worldview. John Wilkins' and G. W. von Leibniz' theories are discussed. The next two essays are analyses of the use of arguments and of truth criteria in religion, compared with other fields in which knowledge-claims are raised. The necessity of an integration between religion and common human knowledge is strongly stressed. The last chapter applies this requirement of integration to a Christian view of history. Many common theological theories are criticised, and an alternative is sketched. The theologians and philosophers considered are O. Cullmann, G. von Rad, W. Pannenberg, R. Bultmann, K. Heim, A. Toynbee, O. Spengler, G. H. von Wright and K. Popper.

Anders Jeffner, Uppsala University, Theological and Ideological Studies, Box 1604, S-751 46 Uppsala, Sweden.

ISBN 91-554-2087-7
ISSN 0585-508X

Printed in Sweden 1987
Graphic Systems AB, Göteborg

CONTENTS

Introduction 7
I. World language and world picture 9
II. Theories of religious language and theological argumentation . . . 19
III. Criteria of truth in theology 31
IV. Christian patterns of history 47

To Fredrik

Introduction

Christian theology rests to a certain extent on faith – faith in the revelation of God. In constructing a theology, we must draw in some sense upon the Bible or part of it as revelation, and rely in part on religious experience and intuition. The Christian theologian thereby claims to have access to a source of knowledge that is not recognized by the secular man. This view appears to be shared by most theologians, and I accept it myself. Sometimes, however, this general outlook is used as an argument for the withdrawal of theological doctrines from trial by ordinary reason.

It is claimed that theologians are bound to move within the theological circle, and that they should not be exposed to disturbance by non-Christian outsiders. This idea is to be found in many different forms, which I do not intend to consider here. What is important for me is to make clear that I am a pronounced antagonist of all notions that theology enjoys a protected intellectual area.

Whatever basis we may have for our theology, we are bound, in my opinion, to demonstrate that our religious beliefs about the world, man and God are theoretically legitimate. This involves at least demonstrating that we can accept our theological doctrines without negating the principles on which we rely in the sciences, in ethics, and in our daily lives. Nor, in so doing, can a theologian be permitted to use other arguments than can be accepted regardless of religious belief. There is, in other words, a basic intellectual meeting-point common to Christians and non-Christians. Every intellectual man who has an important doctrine to propagate must sooner or later come to this point, in order to test his basic standards of rationality, his principles of knowledge, and the consistency of his arguments. There, he must try to show that the principles by which he builds up his total worldview form a coherent whole. When I say that in my view there is such a meeting-point, this is not a simple factual claim. It is to make a basic value-judgment. I find it important to try to establish such a common ground of argumentation. This value-judgment I find inescapable from both a philosophical and a religious point of view. It seems to afford the only possible basis for any real integration within our knowledge of reality, and our reactions to the world in which we live. I see such an integration as a primary philosophical goal. This common meeting-point further means that our religious views will connect with other areas of our intellectual and moral activities. Religion will thus not be an isolated part of our mental activity, a game for our theoretical leisure. An integration of this kind coincides with a general set of values that I find inseparable from any Christian view of life. The aim of this small book is to raise the great theme of theology and integration and throw some light on some of its parts. What I hope to do is to support the theological movement out from the protected area.

My starting point, in Chapter I, is a seventeenth century theory which appears, at first sight, to be a mere curiosity in the history of ideas. It will emerge, however, as a link in an important chain of thought, highly relevant in our computerized age. The function of the essay in this book is to give an unusual historical example of the theological ambition which is its main theme. I have chosen this example for two reasons. The first is a wish to point to the seventeenth and eighteenth centuries as formative for many complexes of problems that have present-day relevance in theology. Further I find it important to pay heed to other theologians than those found in the standard theological text-books when seeking a background to the problems of modern theology. I do not thereby wish to enroll the first secretary of the Royal Society among the great theologians, which he certainly is not. However, other persons mentioned in the article, who generally are labeled philosophers may deserve a more prominent place in the history of theology.

The second and the third essays deal with general abstract problems involved in every attempt to integrate theology into a coherent view of the world. The second concerns the special problems caused by the religious language. What does it mean to argue and to make truth-claims in a religious language? My answer will lead to a new problem, dealt with in the third essay. If you claim to say something true in theology, what are your criteria of truth and how do they relate to criteria outside theology? All that will be offered in this essay are some sketches of a vast area of problems.

Following the general discussion in essays two and three, I will raise in the last essay, a concrete theological problem and try to deal with it in accordance with the integrative principles formulated earlier on. The problem is whether or not there exists a Christian view of history that can be integrated with our secular historical knowledge, and whether this view can add support to a general Christian picture of the world.

The four chapters of this book are meant to be read together, but each is written as an independent essay. Those interested only in one of them can read it separately. The text of the essays is based on lectures that I have delivered on various occasions. In "Christian patterns of history" I draw very much on my Hensly Henson lectures at the University of Oxford, 1981. Nothing has been previously published except a Swedish version of the first essay.

I.
World language and world picture

There are various ways of combating the tendency towards a fragmentation of our knowledge which is becoming, every year, an increasingly obvious problem. Promising initiatives emerge, from time to time, in the course of scientific work, and in the organization of research. But parallel with the necessary scientific integration, I think another sort of integration is needed. This involves work on integrated, overall images for our existence – images that will somehow bind together our various sorts of experience and knowledge, that will offer contexts in the world, and help us to articulate what it feels like to be alive. We find ourselves, here, in the realm of art and religion. But this other type of integration is not isolated from that of the sciences. These different types of search for a whole are interwoven in a theoretically complicated manner. Even historically speaking, they belong together. In this essay I shall be drawing attention to a material from the history of ideas, a material that illustrates various aspects of this effort to achieve a whole, an overall view, an integration of our picture of the world. At first sight, this material may appear to be simply a curiosity, but on closer study it raises numerous questions that are worth our very serious consideration.

A suitable beginning may be for us to contemplate the following text:

I would assume that fairly few people now alive can say what language this is. Those ignorant of Arabic might guess at that language. They would be quite wrong. This text is an example of a scientific universal language constructed by one John Wilkins, and published in 1668. Wilkins is a type of researcher who has played a major role in our history of ideas – including theological ideas – but has received relatively little attention from the theologians. For safety's sake I will offer some data about him.

John Wilkins lived in England, from 1614 to 1672. This was a period in which the natural sciences flourished, and Wilkins himself studied natural scientific subjects. A group of scientists were accustomed to gather in his rooms in Oxford, and from this group there emerged in due course the *Royal Society*. Wilkins was the Royal Society's first Secretary. As a scientist, Wilkins was not vastly original. His first ever publication, however, in 1638, has its amusing aspects. It is entitled *The Discovery of a World in the Moone, or a Discourse tending to prove that 'tis probable that there may be another Habitable World in that Planet*. In a third edition, he added a section entitled *Discourse concerning the Possibility of a Passage thither*. I will not go into further detail on this, in itself, interesting link in the long history of speculation regarding voyages to the moon. The opening passage of this book, however, may be worth quoting as an example of the mood prevailing in Wilkins' environment: "That the strangeness of the opinion is no sufficient reason why it should be rejected, because other certain truths have been formerly esteemed ridiculous, and great absurdities entertayned by a common consent". Wilkins was also a philosopher. In his arguments against the idea that all human endeavour was dictated by egotistical motives, he anticipates David Hume (1711–1776) in a very interesting way. Wilkins was a priest by profession, and became in due course Bishop of Chester. As one might therefore expect, he also wrote theological works. *(Of the Principles and Duties of Natural Religion*, 1678). He believed that the basic features of the Christian doctrine were accessible to reason, and could be developed in a natural theology. This natural theology could utilize the new discoveries of the natural sciences, and show how Nature reflected the greatness of God. This basic theological view Wilkins held in common with the majority of the great pioneers of science. It is to be seen most clearly in Robert Boyle. If we are to classify the theology of Wilkins, we can say that his views are closely related with physico-theology. In its more popular versions, as for example in Derham (1657–1735), this theology displays numerous features which may appear to us ridiculous, but as a whole this enormously influential school of thought is worth a closer historical study – particularly since there is a risk of the historians of theologies interesting themselves more in internal, ecclesiastical squabbles than in the interplay between Biblical faith and culture in the broadest sense. Wilkins' most remarkable book is undoubtedly that from which I took my introductory text. It is entitled *An Essay towards a Real Character and a Philosophical Language*, and it was presented to the Royal Society in 1668. In this Essay, Wilkins offers a new scientific world language, and a new script that reflects the structure of language. Let me describe, briefly, how Wilkins' language is built up. I will then put this description into its historical context, offer a further example of a universal language, and, finally, revert to the complex of problems that I raised initially.

Wilkins' premiss is that the natural languages suffer from numerous defects. They contain ambiguities and lack numerous opportunities for expression. Above all, they fail to reflect a modern, scientific knowledge of the world. The existing scripts are also, in Wilkins' opinion, inadequate. The same sounds are designated with different letters, and vice versa. And the script fails to give clear expression to the structure of the language. Shortcomings like this can be eliminated by a new, scientific language. As a basis for this language, Wilkins tries to present a scientific systematization of all things that can be named – which is to say all entities, both concrete and abstract. His fundamental idea is that there is a natural classification of everything – the same basic idea as could be seen, in Sweden, in Linnaeus. Wilkins arrives at the conclusion that it is reasonable to reckon with 40 primary sets, his word for such a set being a *genus*. The first genus covers the general properties of things, such as quantity and quality. The majority of the remaining genera are comprised of specific phenomena and properties. Examples of these are worlds, elements, birds, and family relationships. Each genus is divided into sub-sets, which Wilkins call *differences,* on the basis of certain properties possessed in common by the members of these sub-sets. Fire, for example, is a difference falling under the genus "element". Below these differences, we then have the individual phenomena that are called *species*. A flame, for example, is a species of fire. Here is another example of the division: genus – sensual quality, difference – colour, species – red. Wilkins applies this classification in the most minute detail, and his book includes page after page of complicated tables, for which he draws upon the natural scientific observations of his age. When it comes to the actual construction of the language, Wilkins does not relate to any existing system of grammar. He assumes the existence of a grammatical system underlying the grammars of all the languages that exist naturally – a natural grammar, to which it is possible to approximate by a new construction. Wilkins reckons with two basic classes of words: *integrals* and *particles*. Integrals are words that designate a phenomenon or a property – the items, in other words, that Wilkins has listed in his system of tables. Particles are different. One important particle is the copula "is". This renders all verbs unnecessary in the language. Instead of saying that someone runs, one ascribes to him the property "running", and so on. There are also particles which indicate number etc. One interesting group of particles is those that Wilkins terms *transcendental*. These change the meaning and references of words. To these particles belong "augmentatives" and "diminutives". If you place an augmentative particle in front of the world "sea", you alter it to "ocean". A diminutive in front of "hot" reduces it to "tepid". There are also particles which alter the meaning of a word to give it a metaphorical import, and others which indicate sex.

Phonetics is a subject that Wilkins attacks with the aid of phonetical dia-grams. Using the Greek and Latin alphabets in combination, he tries to produce non-ambiguous designations for all practical sounds. This, as we shall see, is of lesser importance, and I shall not consider his phonetical system in any more detail.

Against the background I have just outlined, Wilkins shapes his language in accordance with a principle that makes it possible to see directly, from the linguistic expression, where in Nature's system a phenomenon belongs. This is an idea that we recognize as similar to the language of our present chemical formulae. In Wilkins, each genus is designated by a syllable, consisting of a consonant and a vowel. "Element" is "*De*" and "sensual quality" "*Ti*". The difference is then indicated as a consonant. The first difference in each primary set is designated with *b*, the second with *d*, and so on. "Fire" thus becomes "*Deb*" and "colour" "*Tid*". The numbers of the various differences are provided in tables. The species is indicated by adding a further vowel. α for first, *a* for second, etc. "Flame" then becomes "*Debα*" and "redness" "*Tida*". In this way, one obtains in language an image of the natural order of the world.

Phonetic script, which could thus be used for Wilkins' language, he in fact regards as inadequate. He therefore devises an ideographic script which directly clarifies the structure of the language, and thus also of Nature. His principle is simple. Each genus is indicated by a horizontal sign of the following type: ⊥ , ⟋ . These are the signs for element and sensual quality. The number of the difference is then indicated by a specific type of hook on the left-hand side of the basic character, and the number of the species by a corresponding hook at the right-hand end. Fire: ∠⊥ , Flame: ∠⊥⟍ , Redness: ⌶⌣⌶. The particles are placed next to the above characters, in a manner which – like so much else – I intend simply to pass over.

We can now try to read our introductory text, which was the first that Wilkins wrote as an example of his scientific language. In the light of what I have already said, it will be simplest to start with the second character. ⊣ indicates the genus of family relationships. The hook on the left indicates the first of the sub-sets, difference, which is relationship through blood-ties. This can easily be seen in the tables. The hook on the other side indicates species number 2, which designates a person standing in a directly descending line of relationship from someone. The entire character thus means "parent". The first little character is "our", the character for which I will not further discuss. We thus begin to glimpse what text it was that was first translated into the scientific language and put before the Royal Society. It is the Lord's Prayer. Wilkins provides a number of comments to the translation. It would be possible, he remarks, for the sake of completion, to add the transcendental particle indicating that the second word is used in a metaphorical sense. But this, he says, is unnecessary, since it is obvious that this is a metaphor. He then goes on to discuss whether one should not add the particle indicative of masculine gender. This idea, however, he rejects. He appears to be of the opinion that God has been sexually determined owing precisely to the lack of accuracy and consistency from which natural languages suffer. Clearly, a feminist theology appears where we might least have expected it.

The first time I encountered Wilkins' great construction of a world language, I thought it must be a practically unique curiosity in the history of science. But this is by no means the case. The dream of a new, scientific language is an old one, manifested in many different eras – including our own. Nor, as I have already indicated – and this is a subject to which I shall return – is it proper simply to note the curious features of such an enterprise. In the history of artificial world languages, we can discern two main lines. This division is to be found in an early standard work on the subject: L. Couterat, L Leau; *Histoire de la language universelle*, Paris 1903, and the same idea is to be found in a more modern survey: A Bausani, *Geheim- und Universalsprachen*, Stuttgart 1970. The one line comprises an attempt to improve, simplify and develop one or more of the natural languages. We have, for example, the various attempts made to construct a simplified Latin. This line leads to such modern languages as Esperanto. The other line consists of languages that are constructed entirely from scratch, often from the starting-point of a given scientific or philosophical theory. Couterat and Bausani call the first line the *a posteriori* line, the second the *a priori* line. This distinction is clearly made in a letter by Descartes in 1629 (quoted in Couterat, Leau, p. 11 ff.). Wilkins' language belongs to the *a priori* line, which is the only type I am concerned with in my present context. An interesting early attempt to construct a language of this kind is to be found in Raimondus Lullus, in the 13th century. Tore Frängsmyr, a Swedish scientific historian, has written an instructive presentation of Lullus' world language, "The dream of an exact language", in *Vetenskapens Träd* ("The Tree of Knowledge"), Stockholm 1974. Lines can be traced from Lullus back to the Cabbala, and in his division of Nature Lullus can relate back to the interesting 9th century theologian Johannes Scotus Erigena. Further forward in time we find ideas of a scientific world language in such pioneering philosophers as Descartes and Leibniz. Comenius (1592–1670), well-known in the history of education, was also engaged by this idea, as was Swedenborg (1688–1772) in my own country. I will come to some modern examples later. Wilkins represented the acme of the *a priori* line, and he had several contemporary parallels over and above those I have mentioned. Above all, perhaps, George Palgarno (1620–1687).

We can ask ourselves what motives underlie the gigantic task of creating a scientific world language. Obviously, all those undertaking it believe that their new language will facilitate communications between people. Wilkins adds that it will favour trade – a factor that we might seize upon were we concerned to present a materialistic interprestation of history. There is also a religious motive. Man possesses the capacity for a uniform and perfect language, and this is to be developed before the Last Judgment. This view is encountered above all in Comenius. Several others, including Wilkins, lend greater emphasis to the importance it would have for the Mission. It would make it easier to describe the Christian religion to all people, and to present it in such a way that its relationship to the world picture presented by the sciences would be clear. When, however, we study the *a priori* tradition of a world language, we gain the impression, regardless of what the writers concerned explicitly state as to their motives, that the most important motive force behind their gigantic labour was a desire to achieve clarity, an overall picture. Their world language was to help us achieve a better integrated picture of the world.

Before reflecting on any matters of principle, I will take another example from this tradition. I will choose a figure of more distinguished name, the philosopher G W von Leibniz (1646–1716). In the history of philosophy Leibniz is perhaps most generally known for his theory of monads, but modern philosophers have paid attention to him also for his contributions to logic. In the history of mathematics, he occupies an important place. One of his greatest works, the *Essais de Theodicée*, 1710, belongs to the history of theology, but once again the established, intra-ecclesiastical perspective has led to his often receiving but scant attention in this context. A great deal of Leibniz' most important writing consists of notes and drafts that were never published during his lifetime. Most of them are written in Latin. In his notes, we encounter early on his dream of a scientific world language, which he called a *characteristica universalis*. We see that he was referring directly to Wilkins, and he tries to improve on the latter's tables[1]. He comments on Lullus on several occasions, *inter alia* in *De arte combinatoria*, 1666. But he also introduces other lines of thought.

The first step in Leibniz' construction involves the use of definitions to divide up reality, so as to arrive at the smallest component parts of which everything is made up, or the simple ideas in our consciousness. Each simple component – or each simple idea in our consciousness – is then given a name in the language, for example a number. This analytical part of the work is a process parallel to analysing a number into its prime factors. Composite objects in reality are designated in the language by combining, in the same way, the names of the simple component parts. As in Wilkins, the language thus becomes an image of reality. In one text, Leibniz takes a simple example[2]. Assume that an animal is designated by the number 2 and reason by the number 3. Man, who is defined as a reasoning animal is then designated by the product of 2 and 3, which is to say 6. As regards the grammar of his language, Leibniz also to some extent follows Wilkins, for example in regard to the superfluity of verbs[3]. The second stage in the construction of this language relates to the possibility of conducting arguments. Here Leibniz introduces the idea that renders his speculations of real interest. This is the concept of the calculus as an ideal. This concept in Leibniz has in recent years attracted a great deal of attention in other contexts. A calculus is a system of signs that are handled in accordance with certain rules. Even those who have not studied mathematics or logic, have encountered a simple calculus in algebra. The signs in a calculus are of two kinds, variables and constants. The rules are also of two kinds, namely the formation rules which state how signs are to be constructed in order to constitute a meaningful expression, and the rules of transformation which state under what conditions one can deduce one expression from another. We have all, for example, learned a deduction such that from the expression $(a + b)^2$, one can deduce $a^2 + b^2 + 2ab$. The deduction must apply regardless of.the meaning of the variables. The activity of calculating can take place entirely mechanically. Leibniz applied his concept of calculi not only in mathematics but also in logic, seeing the relationship between conclusion and premiss as of the same type as that governed by the transformation rules in a calculus. And just at the point when he is about to shape his scientific language, it emerges what importance he attaches to the calculus. It is to be possible, in the newly designed language, to present all reasoning and argument as a calculus. This provides us with a mechanical method by which we can resolve disputes. Once the language's basic battery of signs has been so designed that the language properly reflects the world, it will be possible with paper and pen to work out who is right in any discussion. Leibniz also dwells upon the idea that machines can take over the task of calculation.

We have seen, so far, that Leibniz uses cyphers and characters in his language. But he also devises a system designed to permit the language to be spoken. This is done by translating the cyphers into syllables, using a simple but ingenious system[1]. 1 is *ba*, the vowel designating the decimal unit and the consonant the ordinal. The decimal unit is indicated as follows: $1 - a$, $10 - e$, $100 - i$, and so on. The consonants thus follow the normal alphabetical order. 10 is thus *be* and 4 *fa*. 81 374 becomes *mubodilefa*. But with this structure the syllables can be arbitrarily interchanged. 81 374 can also be written *bodifalemu*, i. e. $1\,000 + 300 + 4 + 70 + 80\,000$. Leibniz considers that his scientific language will in this way acquire undreamed-of opportunities for expression, and that it can be compared in many respects with music. Wilkins worked on his language systematically, and in detail. In Leibniz we find mostly sketches, pointing to some extent in different directions. This makes it difficult to concretize in detail his dream of a *characteristica universalis*.

No one ever actually spoke or wrote the languages of Wilkins or Leibniz, or of any of their predecessors or successors in the *a priori* tradition. But their work on bringing together all human knowledge and creating a uniform scientific language gave birth to important ideas of overriding scientific signficance, and with a bearing on philosophy and the way we look at life. Let me give, by way of conclusion, some examples of this, with particular emphasis on the philosophical aspects. And by way of a transition to this discussion, I should mention that the idea of a strictly scientific universal language based on a "unified science" played an important role in one of the most influential philosophical trends of the 20th century, namely Logical Empiricism.

What people were aware of at an early stage in the tradition of Wilkins and Leibniz can be described in modern terms as the importance of formalisation for the creation of an unambigous language, with which it is easy to operate. The manner of formalisation that is necessary in the modern natural sciences and in logic constitutes a practical embodiment of the suggestions we have encountered in Wilkins and Leibniz. If they had lived to experience the languages of modern computers, they would have found many of their intentions realized. Leibniz, above all, would find himself at home. We can say that the computers are directly realizing his idea of the applicability of the calculus. But there are points of similarity to be found in quite different topical and wide-ranging areas of science, one example being the idea of an in-depth structure in language. This idea, which we have encountered in the brief survey I have given, is one of the foundations of modern linguistic science, in its various structuralist forms.

Among the relevant philosophical ideas, I should like to point to the picture theory of language. This theory, clear glimpses of which have appeared in my historical survey, implies that the ideal language shall be so composed that its structure directly corresponds to the structure of reality. Each name, for example, of a composite phenomenon shall be composed of the names of the components of the phenomenon itself. In the case of this theory, Wilkins' and Leibniz' modern successors are Russell and Wittgenstein. Everyone who has concerned themselves with 20th century philosophy knows that Wittgenstein, in the *Tractatus,* imagines some sort of ideal language which is a picture of the world, and that Russell's ideas about philosophical analysis incorporate similar lines of thought. Wilkins started by translating the Lord's Prayer, and Leibniz observed on several occasions how useful the scientific ideal language would be to Christian missionaries. In this respect, of course, Russell and Wittgenstein are less than desirable successors. Russell's atheism is well-known, while Wittgenstein maintains that the picture of the world conveyed by the perfect language will not include God. This development in the idea of a world language is due to the fact that the empirical elements present were enlarged upon and refined at an early stage, and also to the sharpening of natural scientific argumentation since the days of physico-theology. The theological ideas that in the early tradition are undeniably blended with the natural sciences and logic in an unreasonable way have not been developed and refined to any corresponding degree. Should we be concerned to attend to this, I think that Bishop Berkeley might provide a suitable link. At all events, the theology has not entirely disappeared in Wittgenstein's *Tractatus.* It is hinted at in various obscure passages which have been quoted to death. Wittgenstein's line of thought seems to be that by working with the perfect language we will cause the limits of that language, and of the world, to appear. Just at the point where they do so, we will have an intimation of something other than the world. The mystical will appear. It is not something we can talk about. To do so would be to draw it into the sphere of the natural sciences. This idea of Wittgenstein's – even if it has now fallen out of fashion in the philosophy of religion – is probably worth reflecting upon by anyone concerned to develop the theological aspects of the world language and world picture tradition. But it is not only the theology in the *Tractatus* that has lost its topicality. It is a well-known fact that Wittgenstein devoted his later philosophy to refuting the view that he developed in the *Tractatus*. Above all, he attacks the picture theory of language and the idea of a perfect universal language. I will not go into the linguistic theory of the *Investigations*, of which many good presentations have been made. I would like simply to offer the reflection that the later Wittgenstein's view of language as a series of distinct and separate games can easily breed the sort of fragmentation of knowledge that the world language tradition was trying to combat. This can be seen with particular clarity in the philosophy of religion that has been inspired by Wittgenstein's later philosophy. This aspect becomes less important if we can say that Wittgenstein, in the *Investigations*, does finally refute the picture theory of language. He undoubtedly makes many interesting observations about language in the *Investigations*, but to regard the picture theory in all its forms as being finally refuted would surely be as naive as it would be to set about constructing a new scientific world language. Among the living elements to be found in the world language tradition from Wilkins and Leibniz, I should like finally to consider their striving to establish, as a basis for the language, an overriding structure in the whole of existence. As we have seen, the principles on which these various languages are constructed presuppose just such a structure. It is worth studying how they set about finding this overriding structure. Wilkins makes the classifying activity which he encountered in early natural science a principle that gives the whole of existence a system. In Leibniz it is instead the logico-mathematical order that provides a pattern, into which he hopes that everything can be fitted. They thus took elements from some individual field of knowledge, which were to lend a structure to the whole. Is this a reasonable activity? I believe so, provided that we at the same time realize that we are leaving the adequate descriptions, and creating symbols, for an integrated experience of the whole. But there are problems here, which cannot be solved directly in terms of the tradition I have discussed. It also appears that such experiences as love, trust and friendship have little significance in the basic structure of existence that appears in all the world pictures in this tradition. No one, I imagine, would wish today to adopt the structurisation of existence afforded by this tradition of thought. But the basic ambition to be found here can offer, I think, a useful reminder in our present cultural situation. We do not, perhaps, need a world language. But we do need a world picture.

NOTES

1 G W Leibniz, *Philosophische Schriften*, Ed. by Der Deutschen Akademie der Wissenschaften zu Berlin. Volume II Berlin 1966 pp 487 ff.

2 *Opuscules et fragments inédits de Leibniz*, by L. Couterat, Paris 1902, pp 42 ff.

3 *De Grammatica rationali*, 1678, *Opuscules* pp 281 and 282.

4 *Opuscules* pp 277 ff.

II
Theories of religious language and theological argumentation

It is common for British philosophers to illustrate their arguments with examples drawn from everyday life in Britain, and from the British university world in particular. The ordinary British reader will, of course, use these philosophers' allusions to everyday circumstances and colloquial speech as an aid to understanding abstract thoughts. A foreigner, however, may often have to go the other way around – first trying to understand the abstract arguments, and then inferring something as to the concrete examples and allusions. It is possible to learn a great deal about Britain and, in particular, about its older universities by such a method, although on occasion it fails to work. In *How to do Things with Words*. (1962) Austin remarks that one of his classifications "is quite enough to play Old Harry with" the value-fact distinction.[1] It was hard enough work to follow Austin's philosophical thoughts at this point, but having made the effort, another great problem remains for the foreigner. What does an Englishman really do when he plays Old Harry? My first thought was that there might be a typical English game, rather like cricket, called Old Harry, even if this would seem a little outré in a Christian country. I studied Austin with great care hoping to learn the rules of the game, and gradually came to doubt that to play Old Harry was a game at all. Now, this illustrates a certain kind of embarrassment – the embarrassment you may feel when encountering something that gives you associations to an activity which is guided by certain rules, but in which the rules are so difficult to observe that you come to suspect that your first associations were totally wrong. I will call this feeling "the foreign spectator's embarrassment".

Let us now turn to theology. It is, of course, necessary for the Church to develop and combine the different doctrines of the Bible and to relate them to other, contemporary thoughts in each succeeding age. For the purposes of theological education, this work must be summarized in books of systematic theology. Many such books of systematic theology have appeared in recent decades, the most influential Protestant example being Barth's enormous *Kirchliche Dogmatik*. Many others are by way of text-books for pastoral training, and most of these seem to be German.[2] To read such a book of systematic theology with a philosophical eye is, of course, to inspect a whole parade of well-known fundamental philosophical problems. This is unavoidable, but it seems to me alarming that certain modern systematic theologies should not only raise problems, but should also cause in many Christian readers an embarrassment. And this embarrassment seems to be of the same kind as the reaction I described just now and labelled "the foreign spectator's embarrassment". We encounter in the stream of theological words something that is very difficult to classify. It gives associations to an activity guided by certain rules – in this case an argumentative activity following logical rules. But the rules are so difficult to reconstruct that one may suspect the first associations to be totally wrong, and the activity to be something altogether different from an argumentation. I believe it to be a fact that many Christian readers will feel the foreign spectator's embarrassment when reading theology; and this is a bad state, whether we are trying to practise the Christian religion or simply want to understand it. Such a confusion is also a bad starting-point for a dialogue with other religions. It also seems altogether unnecessary that theological texts should give rise to this form of embarrassment. After the voluminous discussion that has taken place of the analysis or religious language, we can discern a limited number of ways of understanding religious sentences and religious discourse. Every one of these theories of religious language carries certain implications as to the possibility and character of theological argumentation. Given a specific theory of religious language, it might be possible to say clearly what kind of activity theology is, can be, or ought to be. But very often the theologians do not relate their theologizing to the philosophical analysis of religious language. And precisely this is the cause, I think, of the embarrassment that their theology can evoke. Of course, there are philosophers and theologians who have worked out the implications of their theory of religious language on systematic theology. But it seems to me that there still is a great deal of clarifying work to be done here, and that this is an important field for the study of religious language today. In this paper I will illustrate one of the problems very briefly by discussing an example of theological argumentation, and I will choose an example relating to such classical theological problems as eschatology and the problem of evil. When I speak about systematic theologians, I shall mainly have in mind Protestant theologians, and my example permits me to refer only to a small section of the philosophy of religious language. I shall also refer to this philosophy in a very superficial manner, in order not to make this paper too long and to avoid repeating what I have said elsewhere.

Let us consider two sentences which might be premisses in a theological argument. The first is well-known:

(1) God loves all men.

Of course this sentence is very central in Christianity and no Christian theologian can avoid it. I shall refer to it as "the central God-sentence". The second sentence is the following:

(2) There is a form of existence in which everything happens in accordance with the will of God and finally this form of existence will be the only one.

This sentence, too, is important in the Christian tradition. With very few exceptions, all theologians would agree with it. I shall refer to this second sentence as "the Kingdom-of-God-sentence". It seems at first sight quite obvious that we can use these two sentences as premises in order to draw the following conclusions.

(3) Everyone who participates in the final form of existence will be in a good and happy state.

Let us call this reasoning a logical refutation of the doctrine of eternal punishment. If the two premises are interpreted as ordinary statements and given the ordinary meaning of such terms as "love" and "will" the conclusion is unavoidable according to ordinary logical rules, and I think it quite unnecessary to spell this out. If we add a third premiss saying that all men will participate in the final form of existence, we will have a variant of the argument leading to what is often called an apokatastasis theory. Those who accept this variant must also accept the refutation of the doctrine of eternal punishment. I do not intend to discuss the theological questions relating to this additional premiss, and the doctrine of apokatastasis, in this paper. What interests me now is whether the theologians who accept the central God-sentence and the Kingdom of God-sentence are willing to use them as premises in a logical inference of the type exemplified or not. Some theologians, of course, accept this kind of reasoning explicitly. These include, for instance, John Hick in his book *Evil and the God of Love*. (The Fontana Library 1974) This is also my own theological opinion. But the interesting fact is that the overwhelming majority of modern theologians refuse to pursue this reasoning. Either they deny it explicitly or say that we cannot accept the conclusion with certainty even if the premises are certain; or else they avoid saying anything as to the final state of men, which is a remarkable theological silence. John Hick wrote in 1966 that a growing number of Christians will probably subscribe to reasoning similar to that in our example. But you cannot find any such tendency in the modern textbooks of systematic theology. It is now quite natural to ask what reasons the theologians give for avoiding this argument. But most theologians are not very explicit on this point. To be able to formulate a possible answer, we must elaborate certain suggestions made in their books. In doing this we must relate their theology to different theories of religious language. It is easy to see that certain theories of religious language can be used to justify the theological position by which the conclusion can be avoided, and that there are other theories according to which a theologian who accepts the premises is bound to accept the conclusion. Referring to certain well-known theories of the character of such religious sentences as our premises, we can specify the theological positions according to which the conclusion is unavoidable, as well as the opposite – and more common – position. I think it is worthwhile to do this, and I shall now offer a brief sketch of the two standpoints, and briefly discuss their reasonableness.

We shall find in the process that there are some important types of theories of religious sentences and concepts which do not clearly sustain either the standpoint that the conclusion is unavoidable, or that it is avoidable. A brief outline of these will help us to see certain simple but important tasks that remain to be performed on the borderline between philosophy and systematic theology. My survey of the different theological positions vis-à-vis inferences from the two premisses will consequently be divided into three main parts. First (A), theories according to which the conclusion follows without doubt. Secondly (B), theories which make it possible to accept the premisses and at the same time deny the conclusion. And thirdly (C), some theories which must be complemented with further considerations before it can be made clear whether the conclusion follows or not. Since there is more than one theory in each group, I shall be considering six separate standpoints.

Before sketching these three groups of standpoints, I must briefly mention two opinions which I am going to omit from further consideration; and I must also introduce a distinction. The first opinion to be omitted is that the two sentences which I have labelled the central God-sentence and the Kingdom of God-sentence are totally meaningless. This idea, I think, has been sufficiently refuted. The second opinion is more complicated and less discussed. This is the idea of a specific logic for theological sentences. The first serious attempt to construct such a logic was made, to the best of my knowledge, by the medieval nominalists. Now, I do not find this uninteresting in any way, but I do think it of little relevance to the problems involved in my example. If we interpret the premisses in such a way that the conclusion follows according to the rules of ordinary logic, then we must alter our logic in a very fundamental way if the conclusion is not to follow, given the same interpretation of the premisses. This new logic I suspect to be such a poor instrument of reasoning that no theologian would think of adopting it. When we encounter someone who claims to have a special logical system for theological sentences it is a good rule, I think, to remain sceptical until he has presented his logic in a clear formal way – which must be possible if it is a logical system. Since I have not as yet seen a relevant system of this kind and cannot construct one myself, I will leave this possibility out of the discussion.

In order to simplify my classification I will also at this stage introduce a simple distinction which is often neglected. Sentences like our premisses are often interpreted as parts of a myth or a story, and the sentences can be held to be true statements inside the world of the myth or story. Such sentences can also be seen as containing certain symbols. When we consider the meaning constituted by a literal interpretation of the symbols, or the meaning in so far as it builds up a story or myth, I shall talk about the mythical content of the sentence, using a broad concept of myth. Beside the mythical content there is, according to many well-known theories, a real religious content. It is even possible to claim that a reasonable interpretation can avoid supposing a mythical content, and that we can grasp directly the real religious content. This religious content can be seen as propositional or not, and, as we know, the linguistic mechanism making it possible can be reconstructed in different ways. I must here omit all discussion of this[3]. Now the distinction I was aiming at is one between those who believe, that the theologian should concentrate his reflection on the real religious content, and those who think that there is theological work to be done at the mythical level.

(A) Let us now consider the first type of interpretation of the premisses. It is positions of this kind which make the conclusion unavoidable in an unproblematic manner.

One alternative (1) is to say that the terms and sentences in our example retain their ordinary meaning when used in theology, and, further, claim that by understanding their ordinary meaning we understand their real religious content. Theories of myths and symbols are rejected. Consequently, the theological reflection must concern the real religious content. This is the literalist's position and according to this understanding of the premisses the conclusion is unavoidable. Only very few theologians are willing to defend this position, and I am not going to repeat the wellknown religious and philosophical arguments against it. However, I think this position worth noticing in the present context. People often think that this is the orthodox understanding of religion. If you are orthodox in this way, it is obvious that you must reject such eschatological beliefs as the doctrine of eternal punishment, which are also often held to be orthodox. To accept at once the literalist position, our two premisses, and the doctrine of eternal punishment, is an example of the trivial confusions often to be found in circles calling themselves orthodox.

Another position (2) that we shall note among those making the conclusion unavoidable is constituted by three suppositions. The first is that the premisses have a mythological content which we understand when we take them as ordinary theoretical statements, retaining the ordinary meaning of the terms. The second is that theological reasoning is concerned with the mythological content. And the third is that the reasoning must be logically consistent. The conclusion now follows, but even the conclusion is, of course, a mythological statement. According to this position, the real religious content of the premisses and the conclusion can be interpreted in various ways. It may be a conative impulse, it may be an ineffable experience. The link between the mythical and religious meaning can also be variously interpreted. Does any theologian hold this position? It is hard to say, but it is a possible interpretation of those who deny that we can make any direct proposition about God and still argue with theological premisses. It might be possible to elaborate a reasonable theology starting from this position. But the logically consistent myths of this theology would differ remarkably from the myths in other Christian circles, and in other religions. This could possibly be used in an argument against this position.

(B) Let us now point out as the second category a few theories according to which it is quite in order to accept the premises and deny the conclusion, or to accept both the conclusion and a contradicting eschatology.

The first possibility is to accept a non-argumentative theology (3). This position can be reached if we first accept the idea that theological reflection must concern the religious content of the premises, and then maintain that the religious content is a complete mystery which we can experience but never conceptualize or formulate in words. In the place of the last idea of ineffability we can put another which will also result in the non-argumentative position in combination with a concentration on the religious content in theology; this is the view that certain key-words in the premises, such as "love" and "will", bear a certain resemblance to the ordinary meaning of these words, but that this likeness is totally unknown to us. This idea is very clearly expressed, in English 18th century debate, by those theologians who tried to formulate a theory of analogy without the neo-Platonic ontological premises on which the Thomistic theory was based. Peter Browne, Bishop of Cork, writes "... the particular similitude, and precise correspondency which is the ground of that divine analogy by which we transfer our conceptions and words from earth to heaven, and from man to God; is not only actually unknown, but is inconceivable to us as those divine things themselves which it serves to represent."[4] One of Browne's opponents was Berkeley. In *Alciphron* he points out a consequence of Browne's thoughts which he finds absurd. This consequence is precisely what I have termed the non-argumentative position. Berkeley writes: "You cannot argue from unknown attributes, or, which is the same thing, from attributes in an unknown sense. You cannot prove that God is to be loved for His goodness, or feared for His justice, or respected for His knowledge ..."[5] Now it is interesting to note that the same view of an unknown likeness which can be found in Browne is taken up in a recent work on religious language, Humphrey Palmer's *Analogy* of 1973. Palmer, however, clearly sees the consequence pointed out by Berkeley, and he consequently arrives at the non-argumentative position.

It seems to me that the non-argumentative position in theology can be attractive from the point of view of religious experience. But if you adopt this position, you should not contemplate writing thick textbooks of systematic theology. This view cannot therefore be a reasonable interpretation of those systematic theologians who avoid the logical refutation of the doctrine of eternal punishment.

We shall now point out another alternative open to a theologian who wishes to accept the premises but reject the conclusion (4). He can accept the view that theological reflection should relate to mythological content of the premises, but not to their real religious content. As already indicated, we can leave open the interpretation of this religious content, which is beyond the reach of argumentation. To avoid the conclusion, this theologian must now assume that there are other than logical rules connecting the different parts of the myth. He can see the myth as being built up like a dream-story, sometimes following logical rules, sometimes self-contradictory. It can be maintained that it is precisely the logical and physical oddness of the myth that makes it possible to express in it a real religious content. To develop a myth according to this conception is a process analogous to a painter's work when he combines certain elements from the real world in a surrealistic painting, which can express and evoke very complicated states of mind. I would therefore suggest that we call this position as regards theological argumentation "surrealistic theology". It is compatible with such theories of religious language as Ian Ramsey's. And when a theologian like Emil Brunner talks about the unavoidability of paradoxes in central religious reasoning we can interpret him as a surrealistic theologian. I think, in fact, that this surrealistic tendency is very common in modern theology. Systematic theologians often start by saying that we cannot objectify God or form any concept of the divine existence. In spite of this they reason about God, and their reasoning must then be interpreted as concerning the mythological content of God-sentences. When they accept the central God-sentence and the Kingdom of God-sentence but reject the conclusion, they can be interpreted as subscribing to the surrealistic position. I cannot, however, find an example of a theologian who is surrealist in every part of his theology. Those who speak of a special theological logic may be aiming at the psychological principles that guide a surrealistic theologian in his creative work.

I believe that surrealistic theology is a respectable activity, as is surrealistic art. But if we contemplate accepting it, we must acknowledge that the practice of theology will then have very little to do with either scholarship or research. Systematic theologians are often unwilling to admit this, which can lead us to suspect that they themselves would prefer another interpretation of their theology.

(C) Let me now comment on two examples of theories which we can see as a third category. These have one trait in common, namely that they leave it open for further consideration whether or not the conclusion follows.

I talked in the introduction to this paper about an embarrassment which I called the foreign observer's embarrassment. Now some theologians, such as Paul Althaus, should find it quite natural for certain persons to be confused by theology. To be able to pursue a theological argument you must, according to their theory, be a believing Christian.[6] In relation to our example, this must mean that the key-terms of the premises have a religious meaning that is discernible, but only to believers, and that the theological argument depends on this religious meaning.[5] A believing Christian, but nobody else, can see what follows from the premises. According to Althaus, a Christian theologian cannot use the premises to perform a logical refutation of the doctrine of eternal punishment. Now I try myself to be a Christian, but I cannot grasp this religious meaning which should make the premises compatible with a doctrine of eternal punishment. How shall I know whether the fault lies in my faith or in Althaus's? What are the criteria of a believing Christian? This simple and natural question reveals the weakness of a position that ascribes to Christians a certain special power of theological argument. Such a theory often becomes trivial by using accordance with the special theological position defended by means of the theory as a criterion of a true Christian.

The last view I shall mention in this inventory of alternatives can be termed the "hinting position".[6] It says that theology is concerned with the religious content of the premises, and that the ordinary words used in the premises, although they cannot express this meaning clearly, yet can give us a hint of the incomprehensible mystery of God. We understand the religious content in a very incomplete way, but we can know enough of it to perform a theological argument: This view can be worked out in several ways. One way is the classical doctrine of analogy. The difference between the classical theory of Aquinas and the view we described in talking about non-argumentative theology is obvious enough. According to the classical theory, the similarity in meaning between ordinary concepts and theological concepts is not totally unknown. We can say what kind of similarity it is. However, it has been clearly pointed out that this possibility depends, in Aquinas, on his acceptance of a specific and problematical metaphysics, the most important idea of which is the neo-Platonic scale of being. It is the decline of this metaphysics which has led those who start from analogy to the non-argumentative view. The problem today for everyone who wants to essay a hinting position like the theory of analogy is to explain, without the help of a problematical metaphysics, wherein the similarity of meaning between the ordinary and theological use of words consists. In my opinion, the most interesting attempt to do this has been made by Joseph Bochenski. I would go so far as to say that he has made the only interesting modern attempt to reformulate the theological theory of analogy. This attempt is to be found in an appendix to his book *The Logic of Religion*. (1965). Bochenski's main idea is as follows. Everything we say about God states a relationship between God and the world. The predicates ascribed to God in our premises are consequently to be interpreted as relational predicates, and this is quite possible. But then comes the important step. The relationships we ascribe to God are not the same as those expressed by these predicates in ordinary language. To maintain this, according to Bochenski, would be to deny the transcendence of God. The similarity in meaning lies exclusively in the formal properties of the relations, which can be defined by purely logical functors, for instance reflexivity, symmetry and transitivity. This interesting theory seems to have been influenced by Carnap's ideas in *Der Logische Aufbau der Welt* (1928). You will perhaps recall his example of a description of the network of Euro-Asiatic railways. It is hard to adopt any definite position on Bochenski's suggestion until it has been worked out in detail. Religious language, if we follow Bochenski, will have a clear meaning, and it will be possible to formulate strict arguments containing theological premisses. But I wonder if most religious men do not wish to say more in their theological language than becomes possible with this theory. It would be a very severe revision of traditional Christianity to understand the central God-sentence as a statement of certain formal properties of a relationship between God and man, and precisely such lines of reasoning as are contained in our example will be very difficult to analyse on the basis of Bockenski's theory. This is not a serious argument against Bochenski, since the common Christian understanding of theological sentences may require a revision in order to be reasonable. To work out the logic of theology according to Bockenski's theory of analogy would therefore be a serious and interesting job for any present-day religious philosopher.

If, now, we follow the same general lines as Bochenski, but try to retain a greater similarity between religious and non-religious language, we arrive at our last variant of the hinting position. The specification of such a view would also involve detailed and painstaking work. We would have to take all the religious keywords and key-sentences that have a use also outside religion, spell out their meaning and function outside religion, and then state precisely how much of this meaning and function they retain when used religiously. In our example, we must first say what we mean by human love and what we can expect from a person loving us and then say in what respects Divine love differs from human and how we must alter our expectations. Our example is simple in one respect. It contains terms that are also used outside theology. To take an inventory of the content of theological concepts and statements along the lines I am now describing will become, of course, more complicated when we reach such specifically religious terms and concepts as "omniscience" and "holy". This position can also be combined with a theory of the importance of myths or stories in theology, and in this case the religious interpretation of these myths is to be explained. We must now leave all these problems. But what is obvious, I think, if we wish to follow the general theory which supposes a knowable similarity between religious and non-religious concepts and statements, is that no general theory of analogy or metaphor or language-games, or anything of this kind can free us at one blow from the obligation to clarify each specific case in detail.

The supposition of a known similarity of meaning between religious and non-religious terms, and thus the possibility of arguing with respect to the real religious content of such sentences as our premisses, is common in modern theology and this similarity is generally supposed to be greater than in Bochenski's theory. No theologian, however, has undertaken the work of describing in detail the similarities and dissimilarities, i. e. where the religious silence must begin. Take, for example, Karl Barth. He argues with the help of statements about God, and his arguments appear to relate to the real religious content of such statements. Although he is very cautious, in accordance with his general programme, not to objectify the reality of God, he supposes a conceivable likeness between the ordinary and religious meaning of the terms used to say something about God. When discussing the apokatastasis theory in *Kirchliche Dogmatik* II/2, he seems to accept precisely the same kind of theological argumentation as in our example. An apokatastasis theory appears to follow from his premises, but Barth is unwilling to accept a definite apokatastasis eschatology. His way of avoiding this doctrine as a conclusion is to modify the ordinary meaning of one of the key-concepts of the premises. What he does is to take away from the ordinary concept of love the factor which allows us to say that a loving person *must* do certain things. Our respect for the freedom of God prevents us from saying that God must do certain things, says Barth, who uses the ordinary concept of freedom to describe God.[7] Barth, as we know, devotes a great many pages to his *Kirchliche Dogmatik* but he does still not fully explain the various similarities and dissimilarities between theological and ordinary concepts and statements. His theory of the analogy of faith says no more on this head than that there are certain similarities.

I have now given a brief sketch of six standpoints to a central example of theological argumentation. Each of these views is so formulated that it can be connected with different families of theories of religious language. The two latest open a vast field of clarifying work. Which view of theological argumentation is correct? To be able to make a rational choice, one needs, first of all, an opinion as to the result of a correct analysis of the central religious sentences and key-words. Secondly, we require a survey of the possible positions and their implications. It is this second need I have tried to satisfy in this essay. Thirdly, we must select those positions which are compatible with the accepted theory of religious sentences. These three steps can be taken by ordinary philosophical lines of argument. But for the final choice among the remaining theories, I believe it necessary to appeal to one's own religious experience. Now, a systematic theologian can be expected to make clear how he chooses among the possible alternatives and where the religious experience comes in. But as I have remarked, most theologians are not clear at this point. I have tried to identify, as examples, the essential views of certain theologians. My impression, however, is that many writers in systematic theology alternate between many of the standpoints here listed without even noticing it. A small amount of philosophy could thus have a great effect on the clarity of theology in this field and limit the number of confused readers.

NOTES

[1] I L Austin, *How to do Things with Words*, Oxford 1962, p 150.

[2] I have dealt with this genre in my book *Kriterien christicher Glaubenslehre*, Eine prinzipielle Untersuchung heutiger protestantischer Dogmatik im deutschen Sprachbereich, Stockholm & Göttingen 1977.

[3] See further my *The Study of Religious Language*, London 1972.

[4] Peter Browne, *Things Divine and Supernatural conceived by Analogy with Things Natural and Human*, London 1733, p 5.

[5] *The Works of George Berkeley*, ed by A A Luce and T E Jessop, London 1948–57, Vol III. p 165.

[6] See my *Kriterien christicher Glaubenslehre*, Chapter 5, cf p 64.

[7] K D II/2, p 462.

III.
Criteria of truth
in theology

It goes without saying that the philosophical problems associated with the concept of truth are legion. So, too, are the theological debates concerning truth-questions in religion. I shall not attempt here to offer a survey and evaluation of all these problems and debates. Anyone who attempts to do so in a brief paper will appear either superficial or foolish. I trust that it will be possible for me to avoid the latter alternative, but I am afraid that I shall not be able to escape a certain amount of superficiality on certain points, even if I shall try to delimit my subject very strictly. What I want to do is illustrate and analyse a certain kind of conflict that I believe to be characteristic of the academic theologian who is concerned to say something true in the present cultural situation. To clarify the problem, I must take into consideration certain sociological circumstances that have so far been overly neglected by theologians. Towards the end of my paper, it will emerge in which direction I think a theologian should travel to enable himself to handle the basic theological problems of truth.

The concept of truth

Inevitably, I must start with a few words concerning the very simple and unsophisticated concept of truth that I shall be using in this paper. When we assert, in uttering a sentence in one language or another, that something is the case in the real world, then we are "making an assertion" in the sense of the terminology here adopted. My concept of truth will here be restricted exclusively to such "assertions". This restriction is a very severe one. One of its consequences, for example, is that I shall not be considering logical truth, nor the truth of moral rules, nor what can be meant by such expressions as "true religion", "a true person", and "Christ as the truth". Some of these concepts, however, can be explained in part by using my concept of truth. This holds good, at least, of the last example quoted, namely "Christ as the truth".

An assertion is true when what is asserted is the case in the real world. This Aristotelian definition is meant to be an explication of one of our common, everyday concepts of truth. It does not imply adherence to what is commonly called a correspondence-theory of truth. The "theories of truth" to which the correspondence-theory belongs must be interpreted, in my view, as philosophical attempts to explain what is the ultimate criterion of the truth of an assertion, in the sense stated in my definition. The correspondence-theory says that in the long chain of reasoning which we use to establish the truth of an assertion, we ultimately come back to a comparison between what is asserted and the state of affairs in the real world. The coherence-theory states that we ultimately establish the truth by investigating the coherence of the assertion to a system of other assertions which we believe to be true. I find it quite unnecessary for my present purpose to adopt any definite standpoint vis-à-vis the various philosophical theories of truth. I shall be dealing in the following with criteria of truth that are very much prior in the process of knowing to the criteria dealt with in such so-called "theories of truth". If you tell the adherents of different theories of truth that it is raining, they will all use the same criteria to find out if your assertion is true.

I have one more introductory comment to make concerning my concept of truth. We can never be absolutely certain that any assertion is true. Strictly speaking, assertions are more or less probable. This applies also to theological assertions, and I think we have to agree with Butler's famous statement that "probability is the guide of life". In accordance, however, with an everyday use of language, I am going to call assertions "true" if they are probable enough to guide our lives.

You may be wondering why I have chosen this concept of truth rather than another, say Hosper's concept of "truth-to-life", which applies to works of art.[1] My answer is that the most urgent and difficult truth-questions in theology concern the truth of assertions. If we fail to come to grips with this family of problems, we will never solve any other problems of truth in theology. The reverse, however, does not hold.

The roles of a theologian

With which brief remarks, I will move on to the first main section of my paper. Numerous different, socially defined theological roles exist in a modern university, and in the life of the Church. In doing his theological work, a theologian is bound to play most of these roles. To each role is attached a specific set of criteria of truth. In playing the role, the theologian uses these criteria. Let me illustrate, briefly, the theological roles and their sets of criteria. As we shall see, the sets of criteria belonging to different roles cannot readily be reconciled.

The first social role to be observed is one common to theologians and to most other educated people in our part of the world. We play it when planning our daily lives as members of a society characterized by a science-based technology. In this role, we rely on the scientific theories that have made possible modern medicine, modern communications etc. If my son has broken his arm, I telephone to the hospital, take my car, and drive him there. In so doing, I am accepting many scientific results as a guide to my actions, and in the normal case I will also accept the criteria of truth that have been applied in order to obtain these scientific results. It is not part of this role to deny inductive empirical evidence, or to discredit ordinary empirical testing procedures. Even if we are not scientists, we ourselves use scientific criteria to a limited extent. And many theologians, living as we do in our academic niche of society, are frequently confronted with reminders of these criteria.

Having made these more or less trivial observations, let me turn to a more specifically theological role – that of the Biblical scholar. All modern theologians play this role to some extent, and for the academic exegete it is his main role. In this activity, the theologian employs the criteria of truth common to the humanities. As a result, we know a great deal about the very complicated process that has resulted in the texts we call the Old Testament; we also know that it is extremely difficult to reconstruct an actual history from the apparently historical texts. A closer study of the Old Testament, using the ordinary linguistic and literary criteria, can teach us a great deal about the different stages of religious development in the Near East – a knowledge denied to us only a generation ago. Exegetical studies of the New Testament during the past 100 years have led to numerous controversies, which are well known, but there is also a broad concensus which has entered most text books. To take some examples, St. Luke does not work as a modern historian, and texts like the Christmas Story contain apparent historical errors; many utterances ascribed to Christ by the Evangelists are not authentic; the historical Jesus with all certainty did not utter the command to baptize in the name of the Father, and of the Son and of the Holy Spirit; and St. Paul is not the author of the Epistles to Timothy and Titus. It is not easy to spell out in any detail the criteria of truth applied by the interpreters of old texts. But we all know something about comparative techniques, the weighing of evidence, the analysis of structures, and so on. The criteria involved in these procedures are common to the interpreters of Israelite, Arabic and Icelandic texts. Serious academic Christian exegetes adhere to such criteria, even if with a greater or lesser degree of wholeheartedness. The theological dilemma arising from the fact that some texts claim to be the word of God is something I shall be considering later on.

What has been said of the theologian as Biblical scholar can be applied *mutatis mutandis* to the theologian as Church historian, as a student of the Christian theologies, or as a social scientist in the religious field. To each of these roles belongs a set of criteria which the theologian has in common with his colleagues in other, similar university subjects outside the study of Christianity.

The next social role I intend to consider can be called that of the "doctrinal theologian". In this role, the theologian is assumed to formulate a Christian doctrine, either that of his own Church or, as is the case in ecumenical theology, a common Christian doctrine. He then claims to be saying something true about God, and our relationship to God, or about such important things as the Christian ministry, the Eucharist, baptism etc. It is not always evident from the text-books that the theologians are concerned to make true assertions. However, the normal interpretation of a theologian who works so hard at formulating and explaining a doctrine, must be that he claims to be saying something true about the real world. The circumstance that theologians are bound to models, metaphors, analogies and so on does not alter the fact that they must be taken by a normal reader to be asserting something that is denied, or considered false, by, let's say, a Marxist.

Doctrinal theologians in this sense include, for example, the authors of ecumenical documents. Let me take as an example a document from the Anglican-Lutheran dialogue (Pullack 1972). In German there are numerous examples of theologians who have published books called Glaubenslehre or Dogmatik. Among English doctrinal theologians, I shall be referring to the old and highly influential text-book of Quick, and the more recent one by the two Hansons.[2]

It is not easy to establish what criteria of truth are associated with the role of doctrinal theologian.[3] In that so many different theologies exist, one would expect these criteria to be very different. This is to some extent true, but I believe it possible to discern a pattern common to very many theologians. The most apparent common trait peculiar to this genre is that the doctrinal theologians, when claiming to say something true about God and man and the world, appeal to Scripture. Apart, however, from the Fundamentalists, they very seldom use accordance with a Biblical assertion as a general criterion of truth. They can be interpreted, I think, as reckoning with a "*prima facie* truth of Biblical assertions".[4] This means that a Biblical assertion will be taken as true, provided there are no cogent reasons for its being untrue. It is not part of this role to pay much attention to the reasons for introducing a special theological criterion of truth.

The reasons that are allowed to override the *prima facie* truth of a Biblical assertion naturally differ, but we can find certain common traits also in this respect. Hanson and Hanson state in their introduction that their starting-point is not only the Bible, but also a description of "some part of the history of the particular doctrine in Christian tradition".[5] This they claim to do in a particularly Anglican way, but it is common to all text-books in Christian doctrine either to deal explicitly with tradition or to presuppose the tradi-tional interpretation of a certain doctrine. This use of tradition is not only a way of explaining the Biblical material: it involves for the most part the introduction of a new criterion of truth – and this is by no means restricted to Roman Catholic theology. Even if this often remains unarticulated in Protes-tant theology, most theologians seek to reckon with the principle that can be termed "*the prima facie* truth of the Christian tradition". The Christian tradi-tion can be seen as growing out from the New Testament. This tradition is therefore related to interpretation of the Bible, although it allows theologians to differentiate between truth and falsehood in a way that is impossible if the

Bible alone is seen as a criterion of truth. Many Old Testament assertions, for example, are considered to be true not in their original sense, but in a Christological sense assigned to them by the Christian tradition. This also explains why so astonishingly few results of Old Testament exegesis have entered the text-books in doctrinal theology, or the ecumenical documents. We can take an example of the function of tradition from the theological use of the New Testament. Quick offers us a good account of the Christology of the Epistle to the Hebrews.[6] He appears to assume the *prima facie* truth of this doctrine, and tries to make it compatible with other Christological lines of thought in the Bible. One of the main consequences of the Christological thoughts of the Epistle, is the idea that repentance can only take place once, because Christ died once for all (9:12, 9:26, 10:26). Quick mentions this doctrine, but leaves it without comment. It was set aside by the Church at an early date, and theologians can now omit it from the set of true doctrines by an appeal to traditions. This, I think, illustrates a main function of tradition in all confessions. It acts as a filter, sorting out certain assertions in the Scripture as not belonging to a true Christian doctrine. The appeal made to Scripture in theology is an appeal to certain parts of the Scripture that have been sorted out partly by the tradition of the Christian Church.

How can rational people claim that a given human tradition provides a criterion of truth? Most theologians, I think, would say that the tradition is normative because it sums up a common Christian experience of God, of God as Holy Spirit. Behind such an idea lies the idea of religious experience, or a certain kind of religious experience, as a source of knowledge. It is possible, perhaps, to reduce the criterion of tradition to a criterion of religious experience. In any case, it is quite certain that most doctrinal theologians, from St. Paul on, use the appeal to religious experience as a criterion of truth in theology. This criterion is allowed to modify the claim to truth of Biblical assertions. In Barthianism we encounter an important variant of the criterion of religious experience, even if this school of theology is generally regarded as opposing the appeal to religious experience and relying totally on the word of God. But as all students of Barth know, the word of God is not the same as the word of the Bible. God, speaking to a human being, can make the words of the Bible His own. Man knows that a given word of the Bible is a true word of God, because God, addressing man, gives him the power to know it.[7] This process of knowing, of course, is an instance of religious experience. What the Barthians claim is that it is different from the kind of experience resulting from the natural cognitive powers of human beings. It is a new creation of God, and it makes Christian theology totally different from other branches of human endeavour to arrive at the truth.

I have touched upon the relevance of exegetical results in theology. Let us now ask explicitly: does the doctrinal theologian employ the criteria of truth that attach to the role of the scholarly exegete? Of course he does, to a certain extent. I have noticed that English theologians seem to pay more attention to exegetic results than their Continental colleagues. The application of such criteria means that the truth of certain Biblical assertions has to be denied. However, it is still common among all doctrinal theologians to refer to the Bible without attention to the exegetic criteria of truth. The repertory of the theologians producing ecumenical documents very seldom contains any exegetic truth criteria. The authors of the ecumenical report already mentioned state, as a main point, that baptism in water in the name of the Trinity is instituted by Christ. To start a discussion in this context of the authenticity of this particular word of Christ would have meant lapsing from their role. My impression is that the doctrinal theologian very often forgets the criteria of truth that he uses as an exegete, attaching a *prima facie* truth to assertions which according to a critical historical study of the text are false.

Let me, finally, raise the question of how far the scientific criteria to which we adhere in our daily lives belong to the equipment of a doctrinal theologian. The answer is the same as in our former case: to a certain extent, scientific criteria override the principle of the *prima facie* truth of Biblical assertions. The normal doctrinal theologian does not believe in the truth of Biblical assertions in the fields of astronomy, biology, geology, medicine etc. Sometimes, however, not only the Fundamentalists, but even serious theologians are led to deny scientific medical results that are relevant to certain Biblical assertions. When the question of the miracles of our Saviour, or the bodily Resurrection, are concerned, the situation becomes uncertain.

The role of the doctrinal theologian is not an easy one to play. The areas of application of the various criteria are by no means easy to determine, and their coherence is an open question.

Many main types of theology can be characterised by the stress they put on one of these criteria. A stress on the *prima facie* truth of Biblical assertions produces a theology of the Lutheran Orthodox type. Schleiermacher and the Romantic theologians stress the criterion of religious experience. Those Roman Catholic theologians who draw upon Denzinger in their search for truth stress the criterion of tradition etc. Very few theologians discuss explicitly the meta-rules which are necessary in order to weigh the different criteria against each other; nor do many try to make clear how the limitations imposed upon scientific and scholarly criteria in doctrinal theology influence the use of such criteria in everyday life or in the historical, critical study of the Old and New Testaments.

The last role that I shall briefly consider is that of the preacher. The entire social situation of the preacher forces him to accept the *prima facie* truth of Biblical assertions as his primary criterion of truth. To demonstrate the truth of what he is saying in his sermon, he refers to the text. Many preachers – at least in my country – talk as if this were their sole criterion of truth, and I believe that many members of their congregations see the matter in this way. The preacher verifies his assertions by appeal to the Bible. If, however, we take a somewhat closer look at modern sermons, we can see that in most cases all the criteria of the doctrinal theologian must have been applied to some extent. Most apparent of all is the fact that tradition provides the context of interpretation, although it seldom does so explicitly. It seems to be part of the role of the preacher to disguise other criteria of truth than the Biblical. I cannot avoid the remark that the magnificent term "hermeneutics" is often little more than an excuse for such a disguise of criteria.

Flight from the problems

Many theologians play the four roles I have now outlined, employing the sets of criteria that go with each. This they often do without too much reflection. If these roles are socially well established, the play can continue for some considerable time without disturbing too many people. Sooner or later, however, more and more people must become aware of the problems involved in applying special criteria of truth in theology; nor can the potential conflict between these different sets of criteria always remain latent. People begin to feel that the sermons they hear fail to relate to their ordinary way of thinking in questions of truth, and they come to doubt that doctrinal theology can reasonably be maintained. It is obvious that a situation of this kind is arising in many European countries, including my own.

Those who dislike such a development have special cause to turn a keen eye upon a political trend which at first sight seems to be very friendly towards the Church. I am thinking here of the type of Neo-Conservatism that is now so strong in many European countries. One representative of this trend is Paul Johnson in his well-known book *Enemies of Society*. He accepts those priests and theologians who stick strictly to their traditional roles, but makes fun of those who try to coordinate scientific and religious criteria of truth. Paul Tillich's theology is described as "Christianity without Christ" while Teilhard de Chardin is dubbed a "French pseudo-intellectual".[8]

Before considering, in my next section, the serious theological attempts that have been made to solve the criteria problems underlying this role-play, I should like to point to certain theological tendencies that can be seen more as a sign of dissatisfaction with the situation described than as any endeavour to alter it.

The first tendency is to be found in many text-books in dogmatics. We can call it the flight to descriptivism. Instead of asserting a given theological doctrine, the theologian can simply describe it, adding that this is the doctrine of the Christian Church or of a specific Christian church. To establish the truth of such a description, you need none of the special theological criteria of truth. The truth of the description can be demonstrated by the regular methods of scholarship, and to this extent the theologian is in the same boat as all scholars in the humanities. This, however, also means that he is no true doctrinal theologian. He is not trying to say anything about God, or about our relationship with God. It is possible, of course, to tag on to such descriptions a theory that converts them into theological assertions[9]; but then, all the problems come back. As long as theories of this kind are not made explicit, I cannot help but see the enormous amount of descriptions in the theological text-books as a flight from the problem of theological criteria of truth.

My second example is taken from the field of Biblical exegesis. I said just now that the Christian tradition as a criterion of truth renders many of the results of scholarly Old Testament exegeses theologically irrelevant. Old Testament exegetes who happen also to be Christian theologians have been dissatisfied with this state of affairs. It has been impossible for them, naturally enough, to rely solely on the principle of the *prima facie* truth of Old Testament assertions. They seem instead to have taken the following, somewhat curious route. They adhere to the principle of the *prima facie* truth of New Testament assertions, and consequently believe Christ to be the Son of God, St. Paul's concept of God to be the true one etc., etc. They do not, however, accept such New Testament interpretations of the Old Testament as run against their own exegesis. (For instance that David speaks through the 110th Psalm.) Instead, they try to establish an interpretation of the results of modern Old Testament exegesis that will render their results compatible with the New Testament, except in its way of interpreting the Old. The result is the genre called Old Testament theology. I believe very firmly that the Old Testament has its theological importance, but the way in which Old Testament theology has been worked out from von Rad onwards appears to me, at the level of truth-criteria, to be confused. It constitutes a sign of Christian dissatisfaction, rather than offering any solution to the basic problems.

Attempts to analyse the conflict of criteria

Let us now try to make a survey of the explicit attempts made to analyse the fact that we have different sets of truth criteria connected with different social roles. Insofar as they relate to theology, I think these attempts can be divided into three main groups ((1)–(3)).

(1) According to the first group of theories, different basic human strains of activity exist, in which a given use of language and given criteria of truth are interwoven. We can clarify the criteria internal to each basic activity, but there is no external, more basic point of view from which these can be judged; nor is there any need to coordinate the criteria belonging to different basic activities to make a coherent whole. We have to accept that there is a basic diversification of life, and that assertions are never simply true or false, but only true or false in a certain context. One of the basic human activities is to think and act religiously, and the conflict between different criteria that we often experience can be reduced to an illusory desire to create a unity where none is to be found.

This is the path adopted by the Wittgensteinian philosophers of religion.

This kind of philosophy has been the subject of intense discussion for many years, and I think that many theologians and philosophers are fed up with it. However, I should mention very briefly my own position towards it. I believe it to be impossible to abstract a religious way of speaking, thinking and acting, in which the coordination of different criteria presents no problem. In my view, the potential conflict between different truth-criteria, as illustrated in the roles of the doctrinal theologian and preacher belongs to a Christian form of life. Some Christians have therefore tried, as part of their Christian life, to get rid of this conflict. They have therefore moved towards the third type of theory that I shall be discussing, the one to which I confess myself.

2) Then there is a quite different way of defending the use of special criteria of truth in theology – criteria that cannot be defended from a position outside the circle of faith. This defence is based not on a philosophical theory like Wittgenstein's, but on a religious idea – the idea of some special cognitive ability conferred upon human beings by God together with his word. This cognitive ability makes it possible for men to establish beyond doubt that God speaks to them. It places doctrinal theology in a category quite different from any other human search for truth. This way of looking at theology has a long history, and is by no means restricted to Barthianism. We did, however, encounter one example of it in my previous reference to the Barthians. It is impossible to *argue* against this line of thought. If you try to refute it, those adhering to it can always say that your arguments are irrelevant because the Holy Spirit has simply not given you the necessary supernatural cognitive ability. But even if it is meaningless to argue, we are perfectly free to dislike this theory from a moral point of view, as I do very much indeed. I do not regard it as intellectually fair to claim to have received some supernatural power to see the truth.

(3) According to the third main type of theory, there is a common human ground or intellectual meeting-place where we can discuss and justify the criteria of truth that we use in different areas of our cognitive life. These criteria can, of course, vary for different kinds of truth-claims, but it must be possible to defend them by arguments open to all reasonable men; nor must we ever accept that the correct application of two criteria leads to contradiction. From this point of view, it is a theoretical catastrophe to allow the role-play I have described simply to continue. Among those adopting a favourable attitude towards religion, I think we can recognize three sub-groups (a–c) within this third main category.

(a) The first sub-group consists of theories that solve the problem of criteria-coordination by denying the existence of meaningful religious assertions. If no meaningful religious assertions are possible, the problems relating to their criteria of truth have been completely solved. Among all the theories of this kind, that of Braithwaite can be mentioned as a standard example.

(b) The next sub-group comprises a number of very important and sophisticated theories. Their aim is to show that the criteria used in science and everyday life do not produce a negative result when applied to religious assertions, or alternatively that certain special criteria in the religious sphere can be defended as, for instance, being in accordance with religious or "existential experience". Here we find the entire classical tradition of natural theology, and those modern philosophical theologians who are not Wittgensteinians. I have worked in this field myself, but it is not my intention to leap into the discussion in my present paper. If these theories are on the right line, as I think they are, then the main arguments for the non-cognitive Braithwaitian theory are invalid. Despite having changed my views many times, I still see numerous possibilities of defending criteria of truth such that certain basic religious assertions can be held true, and of doing this without negating the criteria we use in everyday life and in science. As Mackie's latest book shows, the debate is not over.[10] This, however, is a section of theology in which promising work is taking place.

(c) The former group of theories can perhaps create a coherent set of criteria of truth, and rules of application, which we can use both as scientists, and when we say, as theologians, that God exists and makes certain demands of man. But this is poor theology. To get any further, we have to discuss how the principle of the *prima facie* truth of the Bible is to be evaluated against laws based on sense-perception, how the interplay between the Bible and collective or individual experiences is to be coordinated, etc., etc. In this respect, the philosophical theologians offer us little help. Astonishingly enough, even most doctrinal theologians provide only superficial analyses of these problems, as I have already suggested. There is, however, a growing literature on the use of the Bible, written by Biblical scholars who are also Christian theologians; and this can be helpful here. From the English scene, we can mention, for example, James Barr and Dennis Nineham.[11] Such books, or reports like *Christian Believing*, (London 1976) provide a good starting-point for constructive theological work, but much more remains to be done. I would say, in fact, that this is the one field of theology in which a process of clarification is most urgent. In the final section of my paper, I will address some brief remarks to this subject, after I have summed up some of my other points.

The good theologian
and his criteria of truth

If a good theologian climbs up into the pulpit to preach, I think his sermon will consist very largely of other things than assertions about God. He cannot, however, avoid such assertions, for instance that "God loves all human beings". In uttering sentences like this he is claiming to say something true – something that is the case in reality. He is sure that his truth-claim is justified, because he has a set of clear criteria of truth to which he can appeal. These criteria provide the basis for the Christian doctrine underlying his sermon. They are not criteria for use exclusively in the Church, or in the theological circle. They are integrated with those he applies in all the roles of his life, and he is prepared to give reasons for his choice of criteria.

This means that a good theologian and preacher must have reasons, first of all, for the truth of such fundamental assertions as that "God exists", and that the theologian cannot, according to the argument I have just offered, avoid the field of philosophical theology. In that he relies on science in numerous activities in his daily life, he is bound to accept empirical criteria of truth, while denying that sense-experience is our sole access to reality. Referring to the philosophical theology mentioned above, he is in a position to defend some kinds of religious experience as a criterion of truth.

Whether or not this experience is something separate from sense-experience, and just how its cognitive character is to be defended, are questions which I must now leave aside. They have been frequently discussed in connection, for example, with Existentialism, and I have dealt with them elsewhere.[12] What is important to underline is that I am using the concept of "religious experience" in an unanalysed way, while remaining quite aware of the problems involved and the possibility of misusing arguments from religious experience.

Having introduced accordance with religious experience as a criterion of truth, the theologian must coordinate his criteria in such a way that an appeal to religious experience can never render false an assertion based on clear sense-evidence. Sometimes, he has to achieve a balance between the appeal to sensual criteria and that to the criteria of religious experience. There is no mechanical way of doing this. He has to consider, from case to case, how to arrive at a set of assertions which do justice to a maximum amount of his total experiences. I think that moral criteria are of great importance in this process, but it would be beyond the scope of this paper to consider the function of moral criteria in theology.

If we consider the Continental doctrinal theologians who are active just now, it is obvious that Hans Küng's theology has meant a very great deal to an astonishingly large number of Christians of all denominations. One reason for this, I feel, is that he has not given himself dispensation from the basic questions of truth, and that he tries to demonstrate the compatibility of religious and scientific assertions. His philosophical arguments do not make me very happy, but I do believe that he strikes out on his path towards a Christian doctrine in the right way.

Once a theologian reckons with religious experience as a criterion of truth, he can easily defend an appeal to tradition as a criterion. As I've already said, tradition can be seen as a common store of experience. Tensions can naturally arise between traditional and fresh experience, as they do in times of reformation. I think such tension is unavoidable, and there is no objective solution to the conflict to which it can give rise. We perhaps have a parallel case in the field of ethics.

We now come to the decisive question. How is the good theologian to handle the principle of the *prima facie* truth of the Bible? Standing in the pulpit, it is tempting as we have said to refer to the text as the ultimate criterion of truth, once due attention has been paid to scientific insights and the tradition of the Church. But how is he to defend this criterion as a doctrinal theologian? Could he perhaps say that belief in the truth of the Bible is one characteristic trait of Christianity? This is not a good argument. It is precisely what I have called a flight to descriptivism. Could he claim that the *prima facie* truth of the Bible is a self-evident premiss in theology, with the status of an axiom? I doubt very much that many people, on reflection, would feel this principle to be self-evident. The additional problem then arises: What assertions have a *prima facie* truth? Assertions that emerge as the result of modern exegetical studies of the Biblical text? And if so, should it be the assertions contained in the oldest occurrences of the texts, or in the context of the Bible as it was when canonised? Having read most of the modern theologians who are searching for a satisfactory solution to the problems caused by accepting the principle of the *prima facie* truth of Biblical assertions, I have neither found one, nor do I see any possibility of finding one. My conclusion must be that the good theologian has to abandon the principle. There is no Biblical criterion of truth in theology. The books by Biblical scholars which I have just mentioned seem to be arguing along the same line, but I am not sure that their authors have realized how very radical a revision of theological thinking and Christian preaching is here at stake. At least from the standpoint of a Lutheran or Calvinistic theology, the frequently abused term "revolution" seems appropriate. It should be observed that the abandonment of this principle is far more radical than the abandonment of what has been called a "propositional" view of revelation. What is here being denied is even the *prima facie* truth of assertions about revelatory events.

Have I now been saying that a good theologian should leave the Bible to one side in his theology? No, on the contrary; I believe that abandonment of the principle of a *prima facie* truth of Biblical assertions can set us free to use the Bible in a new and fruitful way, and renders the new exegetical results particularly fruitful both to doctrinal theology and to Christian preaching.

The good theologian believes in the truth of many Biblical assertions, but he does this as a result of applying his criteria. He has found in his own life as a member of the Christian community that Biblical assertions are often confirmed by his own experience. He knows that Christ is our Saviour, not because this can be deduced from Biblical assertions but because he has met the living Christ in his own religious life. This knowledge is so overwhelmingly important to him, that he can express it by using the Biblical words "Christ is the Truth".

Let us look at this function of the Bible a little more closely. It would be a gross caricature of the religious life to think of the Bible as a set of assertions confirmed by some kind of independent religious experience. The fact is that the God-experiences of Christians evolve when people adopt the attitudes and patterns of action described in the Bible. A reading of the Psalms, for instance, can teach us to adopt an attitude by which we can experience the presence of God. To behave like the Good Samaritan can open up a new aspect of reality to us.[13] The Bible helps us to reach a religious reality, but it also contains many ways of interpreting and expressing experiences that we may find adequate for our own encounters with God. It also, of course, contains numerous reports of God-experiences in very disparate cultural contexts – reports that we can compare with our own experiences, and that can teach us how manifold the religious life is. These examples, I think, are sufficient to show how the Bible can be of tremendous importance for our religious cognitive life, without being seen as containing any criteria of truth.

It will by now be obvious that new exegetical insights into the variety of traditions in Biblical religion, and into the growth and change of theological ideas, can be fruitful for a present-day Christian. They give him a richer material of patterns and interpretations for his own experiences of God. If, say, the good theologian were to preach on the subject of the Exodus story, he could learn from exegisis that part of it probably stems from cult-texts, which points to one important, and still relevant, place for God-experiences. The text has subsequently been reverted into history. This process has been possible because people have experienced God at work in certain historical events, an experience that is still possible. St. Paul sees the Exodus-event as an illustration of the saving activity of Christ (see for example 1 Cor.:10) – an activity experienced in the sacramental life of the Church. The various experiences that may have been associated with different stages of the text, and are still relevant, can, when taken together lend support to an assertion such as that "God desires community with human beings in order to save them". In my view, a sketch like this can provide far more starting-points for a good sermon than simply taking the text as an historical account that has to be believed, contrary to ordinary historical criteria – an account interwoven with highly incredible and morally suspect miracles.

There is one important phenomenological characteristic of Christian religious experience that I feel I should comment on before leaving the good theologian and his criteria of truth. This is that the transcendent reality is active. In the religious experience, we are not approaching and examining God. It is God who comes to meet us. We are the recipients. This, I think, is what we can express by the term "revelation".

The religious experience is revelatory experience. The good theologian can therefore say that the Bible bears witness to God's revelation. This, however, places a questionmark against the distinction between natural and revealed religion. I believe even natural religion to be based on revelation in the sense described, and that God's revelatory activity cannot be restricted to the Christian religion. What a Christian can claim, I think, is to have received a more complete revelation than those adhering to other religions. He is therefore concerned to tell everyone about this. The good theologian can be a missionary, while retaining great respect for other religions, and without claiming to possess any criteria of truth that men of other faiths lack.

In this paper, I have put great stress on the criterion of religious experience. We all know that religious experiences differ from person to person, and from culture to culture. Does this not lead to a high degree of subjectivity in theology? I think I have to make three closing remarks.[14] First of all, religious experiences must never be allowed to be the sole criterion of truth. They must always be balanced against scientific and moral criteria, in a way that will make it possible for us to do justice to all our experiences, and create order in our total experiential world. Second, there is an amount of inter-subjectivity in religious experience which we must not underestimate. Third, and most importantly, we as human beings have no sure way to religious knowledge. We may desire absolute objectivity in theology, but we will never attain it. It may be appropriate to end a paper on criteria of truth in theology with another quotation from Butler: "Due sense of the general ignorance of man would ... beget in us a disposition to take up and rest satisfied with any evidence whatever, which is real. I mention this as the contrary to a disposition, of which there are not wanting instances, to find fault with and reject evidence, because it is not such as was desired. If a man were to walk by twilight, must he not follow his eyes as much as if it were broad day and clear sunshine? Or if he were obliged to take a journey by night would he not give heed to any light shining in the darkness, till the day should break and the day-star arise?"[15]

NOTES

[1] John Hospers, *Meaning and Truth in the Arts*, Chapel Hill 1946, Chap 6.

[2] Oliver C. Quick, *Doctrines of the Creed*, Digswell Place, 1938; A. T. Hanson and R. P. C. Hanson, *Reasonable Belief*, Oxford 1980.

[3] I have dealt with criteria-problems in modern German theology in my book *Kriterien christlicher Glaubenslehre*, Eine prinzipielle Untersuchung heutiger protestantischer Dogmatik im deutschen Sprachbereich, Uppsala und Göttingen 1976.

[4] Cf. the concept of *prima facie* duty introduced by David Ross. See for instance W. K. Frankena, *Ethics*, Englewood Cliffs, N. J., 1963 p. 23 ff.

[5] Op.cit. p. IX.

[6] Op.cit. Chap XII.

[7] The influential Barthian theologian O. Weber writes: "Nicht nur im gehörten *Wort*, sondern auch darin, dass dies Wort bei uns *Antwort* findet, ist Gott im Heiligen Geist der Wirkende." *Grundlagen der Dogmatik I*, Neukirchen 1955, p. 267. Cf my *Kriterien . . .* Chap. 4.

[8] Paul Johnson, *Enemies of Society*, London 1977, Chap. 9.

[9] This is done for instance by the well-known Swedish theologian Anders Nygren.

[10] J. L. Mackie, *The Miracle of Theism*, Oxford 1982. Cf. R. Swinburne, "Mackie, Induction, and God", *Religious Studies* 19. pp 385–391.

[11] James Barr, *The Bible in the Modern World*, London 1973. James Barr, *Explorations in Theology 7*. London 1980. Dennis Nineham, *The Use and Abuse of the Bible*, London 1976.

[12] See for instance "The Relationship between English and German Ways of doing Philosophsy of Religion", *Religious Studies* 15, pp 247–256 and "Religion and Understanding". *Religious Studies* 17, pp 217–225.

[13] See further the comments on H. H. Price's view of religious experience in my *The Study of Religious Language*, London 1972, pp 110–112.

[14] Cf. Hanson and Hanson op.cit p. 6.

[15] From the sermon "Upon the Ignorance of Man". (*The Works of Bishop Butler ed. by J. H. Bernard, Vol. I, London 1900 p. 195 f.)*

IV.
Christian patterns
of history

Christian views of history have played an important role in our theological tradition from St. Augustin onwards, and many modern theologians, such as Cullmann, say, or Pannenberg, place enormous emphasis on this theological theme. It is so widely dealt with in modern theology, that we have numerous anthologies devoted to it. These Christian views of history are members of a larger family of ideas, which I will call "metaphysical patterns of history".

Examples of such patterns, lying outside the theological tradition, are to be found in Toynbee's huge and well-known work *A Study of History* (1934–54), in Oswald Spengler's *Untergang des Abendlandes* (1922), and in historical material-ism. Hegel's philosophy of history, deeply involved in both philosophical and theological tradition, can be taken as a paradigmatic example. The theories just exemplified all belong to what Popper calls "historicism". It is far from clear, however, what properties, according to Popper, make historical theories "historicism". A very central characteristic of certain theories which Popper classifies as "historicist" is that they contain long-term prognoses of historical development.[1] This is true, for example, of Spengler's theory.[2] But Toynbee – whom Popper quotes as a key example of historicism – denies several times and in very strong terms that his theory of historical development can provide the basis for any long-term forecasts.[3] There is, moreover, no agreement among philosophers as to the reasonableness of accepting metaphysical pat-terns of history, or "historicist" theories. Popper's main concern is to show that they are serious and dangerous mistakes. However, a critical philosopher and logician such as G. H. von Wright has found much of philosophical and cultural importance in such obvious historicists as Spengler and Toynbee.[1]

Against the general theological background which I have now outlined, it must surely be of central interest to define clearly the set of theories to which the Christian patterns of history belong, and to ask, first, if a theory belonging to this class can reasonably be asserted at all, and, second, if so whether a Christian pattern, in particular, can be defended. This is what I intend to do, and I will start with the question of definition.

To arrive at the first common characteristic, it may be helpful to consider a concrete problem of historical explanation. Let me choose one from the history of theology. Being a Lutheran, I recognise, naturally, that Luther had many deep religious and ethical insights, from which we have a great deal to learn. Everyone, however, who studies his works will also find that he emerges, towards the end of his life, as a crude anti-Semite. I am thinking here in particular of his *Von den Juden und ihren Lügen*, published in 1543.

This is one of the most deplorable anti-Semitic pamphlets ever written. A problem of historical explanation here arises: how could a man like Luther publish this crudely anti-Semitic book?

One possible way of explaining Luther's anti-Semitism is to investigate his personal psychological development.[5] We will then discover that he had a domineering father, his relationship to whom was problematic. Given existing psychological theories of how the authoritarian personality develops, and the connection between such a personality and racist attitudes, we might arrive in this way at a plausible psychological explanation of Luther's anti-Semitism.

But we could also follow an entirely different line. An investigation of the social situation of the Jews in German society might reveal that they constituted an economic threat to the ruling classes of the small principalities. Luther, who was allied to those classes, might be reflecting, in this book, a social tension. This we can call a socioeconomic explanation.

Many historians of ideas would try to explain Luther's anti-Semitism against the background of his general belief-system and theological ideas. They might observe the dark traits in his image of God, and the dialectics between love and evil that characterises part of his thinking. This kind of explanation we can label ideological or "belief-related".

The problems of historical explanation are much discussed in contemporary philosophy, and it is not my intention to focus on this field at all. I wish only to deal with the three *types* of explanation, exemplified by way of illustration. I believe that each type of explanation can be supported by empirical material, and worked out in a way that renders it plausible. The three types are also logically compatible, and it is possible to add them in order to arrive at a complete explanation. In cases such as this, however, we often wish to establish also which type of factor is the most important. We make a gradation of the different types of explanation. Ernest Nagel has argued that we can in some cases arrive at such a gradation on a strictly scientific basis,[6] but in the case of unique historical events I think this is impossible in practice. However, precisely the general theories of history that I mentioned earlier on function in such a way as to provide a gradation. They draw attention to one class of explanatory factors as being particularly important, in that these factors, according to the theory, are connected with the core of historical development. In any Marxist explanation, for instance, the socio-economic explanation becomes the most important. In Hegel's philosophy of history, the belief-related explanation deserves special attention. This gradation can be arrived at by two different kinds of reasoning. According to the first, the various explanatory factors can be reduced to a single kind of factor. Psychological and belief-related factors, for example, can be reduced to socio-economic factors. Or socio-economic and belief-related factors to psychological factors. In the latter case we have the theory that Popper calls "psychologism". But it is also possible to take a general pattern of history as a basis for stressing one particular kind of explanation, without resort to a reductionist argument. This seems to be the case in Toynbee's work. He finds, towards the end of his work, that the development of religious ideas is a key to historical development, but he does not, as far as I can see, take the reductionist step.

This long walk over a philosophical mine-field has now led us to what will be our first defining characteristic of a metaphysical pattern of history. Such a pattern makes a gradation of different types of explanatory factors, and this it can do in two different ways:

    (a) in a reductionist way, and

    (b) in a non-reductionist way.

We can now proceed to a function which is easier to discern, and also more important. In many textbooks, we find an illustration of historical materialism in the form of a staircase. The first step is the primitive community, the next is the slave-owning community, and so on. The final step is the Communist society. It emerges immediately from this picture that the theory illustrated aims at giving a total view of the historical process – an all-embracing Gestalt. The second defining characteristic of a metaphysical pattern of history is that it gives an all-embracing Gestalt of history.

In Spengler and Toynbee, this process of arriving at a Gestalt is achieved in two steps. First they discuss a specific unit, which Toynbee calls civilisations. Second, they find a pattern that characterizes these units. Spengler's theory is the less complicated. The civilisations – he calls them cultures – all follow a cyclical development, and they can be seen in analogy with organisms – an idea common in the Western history of ideas.

My use of the psychological term "Gestalt" is not accidental. The process here involved appears to be precisely the formation of a Gestalt. The various historical facts are arranged into a whole, and this whole lends the individual parts a new significance. We must now, however, draw attention to a dividing-line between two different kinds of Gestalt. The Marxist staircase model is such that the Gestalt embraces the future. To close the Gestalt, we must imagine that future development follows a specific course. The same is true of the idea of historical organisms. For Spengler, the decline of the West is given by his way of forming a Gestalt. We can thus distinguish between formations of this kind that are (a) future-inclusive and (b) not future-inclusive. In the case of future-inclusive Gestalts, their formation is dependent on a belief that certain events will take place in the remote future. A Gestalt that is not future-inclusive can naturally influence very deeply our view of the future, and our expectations, but it is not built on suppositions concerning the future course of history.

It is very important to observe that the historical Gestalts are connected with our values and attitudes. The way in which we form a Gestalt can be affected by the values to which we give priority – for example social justice. And a given evaluation can be supported by the way in which we order history. We must note, particularly, what we can call our "basic emotional experience of life". I am thinking here of an abiding experience or mood which can accompany our whole life. The most simple example would be pessimism, or optimism. A basic emotional experience of this kind can deeply affect our formation of a Gestalt, and, conversely, a Gestalt can help to maintain that experience.

We are in a position to study, in a process that is taking place just now, how a change of value-pattern affects the Gestalt found in history. I am thinking here of the intellectual work taking place within the feminist movement. To the feminists, the suppression of women is a major injustice. A primary goal is the liberation of women, and the development of a feminine basic experience of life. In connection with this, some feminists have developed a new understanding of history. They have formed a new Gestalt. In the foreground are the matriarchal and patriarchal structures, and the tensions between these. Some people have developed this into a theory of an *ur*-matriarchy, from which our present society is a disastrous Fall.

Were we to look for examples of connections between evaluation and Gestalt in the Western history of ideas, I am sure that we could make many interesting observations, but this would lead us too far afield. Let us simply note, as a third characteristic of metaphysical patterns of history, that they support and express a basic emotional experience of life, and a value-structure.

The values concerned can vary in many ways. But we shall be in a position to discern one important value-pattern if we consider, to begin with, a reflection made by Hegel in his lecture on the philosophy of history.[7] He observes there that the metaphysical patterns of history – including those that are non-religious – are by way of being theodices. It is shown, through the pattern, how evil and apparently meaningless events in history acquire a positive value as they fall into place within the overall Gestalt. It can be maintained, for example, that the pain and suffering which appear to afflict a man unmeaningfully are important in that they are leading history towards its goal. Or that the destruction of an entire group of men is a "good thing" when seen from the perspective of the whole. They were perhaps obstacles in the path of historical development. It is important that we should try to clarify the value-judgments at work here. In many cases, I think, we see a principle which I will term an "instrumental evaluation of men". Let the letter G stand for a good state of affairs, and P for a person. The principle then says: "P's life is meaningful and valuable if it contributes to the realization of G, regardless of whether P will or will not share in G, and of whether P recognizes or does not recognize G to be a good state". Marxist historians, for example, say that Luther's life was meaningful and good because it promoted the historical development towards a Communist society. Luther, of course, did not enjoy the fruits of such a society, nor, we may be sure, would he have wanted to. We can now sub-divide also our final characteristic into an (a) and a (b). (a) is a value-structure that includes an instrumental evaluation of men, and (b) is one that does not include an instrumental evaluation of men.

We are now ready to formulate a definition of our key concept.

A *metaphysical pattern of history* is a theory about the course of history, the function of which is

(1) to give a gradation of types of explanatory factors in
    (a) a reductionist way, or
    (b) a non-reductionist way, and

(2) to give an all-embracing Gestalt of history, which is
    (a) future-inclusive, or
    (b) not future-inclusive, and

(3) to support and express a basic emotional experience of life, and a value-structure, which
    (a) include an instrumental evaluation of men, or
    (b) do not include an instrumental evaluation of men.

In each of these three points, we have drawn attention to a line (a), and an alternative line (b). The metaphysical patterns of history which follow line (a) we will term *hard metaphysical patterns of history*, and those which follow line (b) we will term *soft metaphysical patterns of history*. A theory that follows line (a) in one respect will generally do so also in the others. It is, however, possible for a metaphysical pattern to be hard in one respect, and soft in another. The connection between the three defining characteristics is not, of course, one of logical consequence. Nor, however, is their interrelationship purely psychological. Let us say, for example, that you have adopted a given position on point (2). This can then be used as an argument in favour of standpoints in the other cases. A (b) position on point (2), for example, can be used as an argumentative ground for (b) positions on the other points. If you claim, in (2), to know the end of history, then it will be easier to defend an instrumental evaluation of men. From the argumentative point of view, the position adopted in (2) seems, in fact, to be a key position.

If we could arrive at a good and reasonable metaphysical pattern of history, this, naturally, would be of great importance. The first property of such a theory could steer the direction of historical scholarship, and add acumen to our search for historical explanations. A Gestalt in the chaotic mess of historical events would be of major intellectual importance. We would acquire an order in our experiential world, and better means of orientation in our reality. The third characteristic property of a good metaphysical pattern of history could help us to a more adequate emotional experience of life, and support our ethical endeavours.

Until now, I have deliberately chosen my examples more from the philosophical than from the theological tradition. This in order to demonstrate that the problem of metaphysical patterns of history is much more than an internal, theological concern. A moment's reflection, however, will make it clear that the main source of metaphysical patterns of history is, in our situation, the Christian tradition. It is frequently observed that the Biblical tradition has deeply influenced the way in which we evaluate and structure history. In this field, our heritage from Jerusalem is commonly regarded as much stronger than that we have from Athens. From the time of St. Augustine onwards, the entire philosophical tradition of the West has been inspired by Christian ideas. The main exception seems to be Nietzsche's theory of eternal rebirth. Among present-day theologians it is easy, as I have already remarked, to compile a long list of influential thinkers who have focused on the problems of history, and thereby elaborated Christian metaphysical patterns of history. A decisive question for the theologian in this situation must be this. "Is a good metaphysical pattern of history to be found in the Christian tradition?" My approach to this question will be to focus on the main arguments brought to bear against metaphysical patterns of history, and then try to see to what extent they damage the Christian alternatives.

Let me start with a well-known argument, aimed at the heart of all metaphysical patterns of history. It is obvious that such views of history involve certain cognitive claims. These cognitive aspects, it is argued, are not open to any kind of disproof by historical or other research. They therefore lack meaning, and have false pretensions. This is a standard argument in the empirical tradition, and it is carefully elaborated in the field in question by Popper. It has been so widely discussed that I can deal with it briefly. It is obvious that metaphysical patterns of history are not exactly similar to scientific theories, or the result of empirical historical research. That is why I have called them metaphysical. The question of their disproof is therefore not the same as in the sciences, or in ordinary scholarship. This, however, far from settles the question of their legitimacy. In defining the theoretical core of metaphysical patterns of history, I have stressed the formation of a Gestalt. I hope thereby to have made it clear that metaphysical patterns of history are based on an intellectual activity that is perfectly legitimate, even if it may produce a variety of results on the same basis of empirical facts. Popper recognizes this clearly enough. If, however, we are to claim that the historical facts can be held together in a certain Gestalt, this claim cannot be unaffected by our factual historical knowledge. The upholding of a given Gestalt can entail the denial of certain apparent facts. In this case the Gestalt can be said to be inadequate, or, if you like, falsified. Also, a given Gestalt may be built only on a narrow section of the relevant facts, omitting large areas of history. If the area neglected is very large, then the Gestalt must be taken to be irrelevant, or of lesser interest. Let me sum up this argument. A metaphysical pattern of history is based on a well-known and unavoidable theoretical activity. Observing this characteristic trait of metaphysical patterns of history, we see that they are none the less open to testing procedures, and can be shown to be at least inadequate, if not absolutely false. The standard argument adduced against their cognitive meaning thus cannot destroy them at a single stroke.

What I have so far said about testing can now be used to formulate two criteria of a "good" metaphysical pattern of history. (1) It must be compatible with the historical facts. (2) Its application must not result in large gaps. There is much more to be said on this subject, and I will return to the important point of testing later on. For the moment, however, I would prefer to elaborate on what I have already said, by discussing a theological example. Let us take a common metaphysical pattern of history in the Christian theology, and apply the two very simple criteria, which we have formulated in our defence against the first argument.

The Swiss exegetic theologian Oscar Cullman published, in 1946, his book *Christus und die Zeit*. (*Christ and Time*, London 1951) Many theologians – especially those critical of Existentialism – have been influenced by it. Bultmann criticised Cullman in a well-known review,[8] but Cullmann has subsequently restated and elaborated his view in *Heil als Geschichte* (Tübingen 1965)

Cullmann claims that a specific concept of time and history is very important in the New Testament, and that it provides the background to the doctrine of salvation. The theory of time and history that Cullmann constructs from his New Testament studies is, in our terminology, a metaphysical pattern of history. It is far from clear how much of this pattern Cullmann thinks that present-day theology can take over. He makes certain reservations regarding the concept of time, and introduces a distinction – foreign to the New Testament – between history and myth. One gains, however, the impression that the New Testament scheme that Cullmann claims to have discovered should be adapted, by and large, by modern theology. This impression is confirmed by his *Heil als Geschichte*. It is from this aspect that it is of interest in our argument.

Let me give a brief summary of Cullmann's view. Time is seen as a linear process, a limited section of which is occupied by the development of our own world. There is a time prior to the Creation, in which God is working out his plans for the world. The Creation is followed by the period covered by primeval history. Cullmann says that the New Testament writers saw this as ordinary history, but when we, who in contradistinction to them have the concept of myth, call it "mythological", we have to reckon with a period of time subsequent to the Creation but beyond the reach of historical research. This we can do as Christians, on the basis of revelation. The decisive event during this period must have been the Fall. The historical period is structured by God's election of His people as a representative of mankind. Within this people, a process begins that narrows down this representation first to a remnant and then to Christ. In Christ, as a representative of mankind, God wins his decisive victory, and with Christ a development commences towards the inclusion of all people in the salvation history. Christ's victory becomes apparent in the Parousia, after which eschatological time begins. Schematically, the process is something like this.

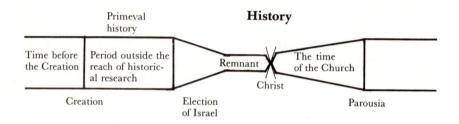

Those who criticize the exegetical basis of this theory appear to me to have many good arguments, but it is not my intention to discuss the exegetical aspects. Neither am I going to discuss the naive concept of time here involved. As I have already said, Cullmann himself realizes that it is theologically problematic. I shall be returning to similar problems later on.

Let us now concentrate on the structure assigned to history by this theory, using the two criteria at which we have arrived.

The first question is whether acceptance of this pattern leads to conflicts with any of the historical facts. The most problematic point in this respect is the time subsequent to the Creation but prior to recorded history, a period that is decisive for the formation of Cullmann's Gestalt. Cullmann states that events during this period cannot be verified by historical research. To claim on the basis of revelation that something has happened in the world which is historically unverifiable may be possible in theology. But that does not help us very much in this context. The real question is whether the factual claims made are capable of disproof, and this discussion is very much neglected by Cullmann. The idea of a period in the development of mankind during which certain morally significant events occurred is very difficult to filt into the known sequence of development of the human race on earth. To assume such a period is not only to accept a hypothesis that it is impossible to verify, but also one that runs counter to all the hints that are left to us from the youth of mankind. As far as I know, we cannot definitely disprove the existence of such a period, but it seems so improbable that to claim its existence constitutes a threat to the ordinary principles by which we set about establishing facts about ancient periods of time. In this case, the theological assertions made become very dubious, given the basic theological view that I sketched in my introductory remarks.

It seems to me, by way of conclusion, that Cullmann is offering a half-way de-mythologization of primeval history, as a result of which his pattern of history fares badly when exposed to the ordinary trials of evidence and logic.

Let us now apply our second criterion. Does this pattern cover the entire historical process, or is a great part of it left outside the pattern, without a Gestalt? The latter seems obviously the case. Nothing whatsoever is said of the many thousand years of human history that preceded the emergence of the Israelite people, except that all men were in need of salvation. The tribes living at the dawn of the human race, the great cultures that subsequently developed in different parts of the world, are in this scheme simply heathendom. Neanderthal Man, Confucius, Aristotle, all are assigned to the same category. The current development of world history is structured from the perspective of the Christian mission, and such a phenomenon as the emergence of the Islamic culture is not worth mentioning in this scheme. I am bound to conclude that this metaphysical pattern contains such great gaps as must necessarily render it unsatisfactory.

I have claimed, in rejecting the first general argument against metaphysical patterns of history, that they are in fact partially open to empirical testing. We have seen now how this advantage can present a Christian pattern with serious problems. I did not choose Cullmann as a random example. I believe him to be the most representative of a whole family of Christian beliefs about history. These are generally held to be in some sense orthodox, and are often less protected than Cullmann's against disproof in the field of primeval history. I would conjecture that all these seemingly orthodox theological relatives of Cullmann's have greatly contributed to his popularity. The critical remarks I have made up to now are certainly relevant to a very broad body of Christian doctrine. As we proceed in our discussion, we will encounter many more arguments against this cluster of ideas, of which Cullmann has provided us with our first example.

Let us now return to the general discussion of metaphysical patterns of history. One of Popper's main arguments against historicism is that long-term categorical historical prognoses or prophecies are impossible. Popper's arguments are directed mainly against theories that aspire to offer scientific prophecies, i. e. to have arrived at scientific laws governing historical development. Now that the discussion of Popper is waning, I think it only fair to admit that his arguments on this point have remained largely unanswered.

The strongest version of Popper's argument is that given in the Preface to the second edition of *The Poverty of Historicism*. Starting from the fact that we cannot predict, by rational or scientific methods, the future growth of our scientific knowledge, he arrives at the conclusion that we cannot predict the future course of human history. This he calls a refutation of historicism, but it is obviously not a refutation of all the theories covered by our term "metaphysical pattern of history". On the bases of Popper's arguments, we might conclude that any metaphysical patterns claiming to base a Gestalt of the future on rational or scientific grounds must be rejected. But what about those Gestalts of the future which claim to be based on revelation? In the theological perspective, these constitute an important group. It is from such theories that Popper has borrowed the very concept of a prophecy. They cannot be refuted by Popper's argument against rational predictions. Theological theories assume a Higher Intelligence, who knows the limits of human endeavours and who communicates with man. Given this premiss, can we defend a given Gestalt that embraces future history? In discussing this point, we must distinguish between two types of forecast.

The first type consists of forecasts about certain decisive events in the future – the fall of Jerusalem, the appearance of an evil world-ruler, or the founding of a "millenium". These are held to be revealed, because they are based on the Bible. This kind of prophecy is not today common in academic theology, but it still lives on among many Christians – even outside the apocalyptic sects. Nobody, I think, can doubt that it is a well-established part of our religious heritage. How, then, shall we evaluate it? Since we cannot know *a priori* that these prophecies really are an adequate revelation from the all-wise God, there seems no way out but to try to establish how far detailed Biblical prophecies relating to what is by now past time have proved to be correct. This, I am afraid, will give very negative results. One of the most central of the detailed prophecies contained in the New Testament concerns the Second Coming of Christ. There is no doubt but that many New Testament writers are claiming knowledge that this most decisive event will be taking place within a fairly short space of time, and we know that they were wrong. Since the time of Albert Schweitzer, the implications of this fact have been much discussed. It is seldom, however, raised when discussing the reliability of New Testament prophecy. I think, however, that we are obliged to follow this road, even if it is not a very comfortable one for the traditional Christian. We could quote numerous other examples of short-comings, but it is difficult to find a single clear and indisputable example of success in this kind of prophecy. We are bound, I think, to draw the conclusion that Biblically based prophecies regarding clearly defined future events are not reliable, and cannot be ascribed to revelation.

There is, however, also a second kind of forecast, and a much more sophisticated one. It is claimed that the meaning of history, and its total Gestalt, will emerge when the historical process is finished. It will be apparent, from the end of history, what the goal of the entire process was. We, however, as Christians have a foreknowledge of this final goal through Christ. We therefore know something more about future history. We can anticipate the final glimpse of our total history. This kind of future-oriented theology is to be found, for instance, in the writings of Pannenberg.

A temporal eschatology seems in fact to be becoming popular again in many theological circles, as a reaction to Existentialism. We encounter numerous theories about the end of history, or theories of history seen from its end-point. But is this a consistent idea at all? If a person living in our world discovers, in some mysterious way, that the end of human history is close at hand, then this person is still inside history. He is still part of it, and he cannot know whether something absolutely unexpected will happen at the last second. Let us imagine that there are human beings living after the destruction of this universe. They must be incorporeal beings, or beings with a totally new kind of body, having sources of knowledge utterly inconceivable to us. Whatever may appear to them about human history must lie outside anything we can imagine. To anticipate the viewpoint of such beings seems absolutely impossible. When I think along these lines, I must confess that the idea of seeing history from its end-point seems to me confused.

The conclusion to be drawn from all I have said about prognoses and prophecies is that the problems involved in foreseeing the distant future in any categorical way are extremely great. This cannot be made into a conclusive argument against metaphysical patterns of history, but it does argue in favour of those patterns which are not future-inclusive.

We are now ready to turn to the third kind of critical arguments directed against theories belonging to our category. These are the ethical arguments. Speculative historical theories are said to offer a foothold to authoritarian attitudes and anti-democratic forces. Again, Popper is the leading critical philosopher, but I am not going to discuss in any detail *The Open Society and its Enemies*. I think that metaphysical patterns of history can have, and have had, bad social och ethical consequences, and above I drew attention to what to my mind is the decisive point here. It is the principle which I called the instrumental evaluation of men, and which was as follows: "A person's life is meaningful and valuable if it contributes to the realization of a good state of affairs, G, regardless of whether the person in question will or will not have a share in G, and regardless of whether he regards or does not regard G as a good state of affairs". Not only minor injustices but the most hideous cruelties can be defended on the basis of this principle. The alleged laws of history, or the expected great goal of history, render individual human beings fairly unimportant. Human beings can be justly sacrificed to achieve the overall goal. Not overmuch reflection, I feel, is required to see the dangers of the instrumental evaluation of men, and a good metaphysical pattern of history will necessarily be of the kind that does not include this principle.

Let us now turn to the theological theories of history. Do they contain an instrumental evaluation of men? When first confronted with this question, I think that many Christians would say no. We are used to seeing Christianity as an anchorage of individual human value. Unfortunately, however, I think we are bound to confess that some Christian views of history offer a very solid foundation for an instrumental evaluation of men. One of the best-known passages in the Old Testament, in the Christian tradition, is the calling of the Prophet, in Isaiah 6. We have all, I think, been accustomed to see this message from the positive side. The pattern of salvation history is emerging. But we must now observe also the other side – the idea of numerous people being sacrificed for the goal to be accomplished. God is undoubtedly here portrayed as employing an instrumental evaluation of men. God speaks to Isaiah:

> Make the hearts of this people fat, and make their ears heavy, and shut their eyes; lest they see with their eyes, and hear with their ears, and understand with their heart, and convert, and be healed.

> Then said I, Lord how long? And he answered, Until the cities be wasted without inhabitant, and the houses without men, and the land be utterly desolate.

> And the LORD have removed men far away, and there be a great forsaking in the midst of the land.

> But yet it shall be a tenth, and it shall return, and shall be eaten: as a teil tree, and as an oak, whose substance is in them, when they cast their leaves: so the holy seed shall be the substance thereof.

Another Biblical story which is often said to have had paradigmatic importance for the emergence of the Judeo-Christian sense of history can, similarly, serve as a foundation for an instrumental evaluation of men. I am thinking here of the Exodus narrative. When Luther is arguing against Erasmus, he quotes as a key text the passage in which "the Lord hardened Pharaoh's heart" (10:27). In Chapter 10, God says to Moses:

> Go unto Pharaoh: for I have hardened his heart, and the heart of his servants, that I might shew these my signs before him:

> And that thou mayest tell in the ears of thy son, and of thy son's son, what things I have wrought in Egypt, and my signs which I have done among them; that ye may know how that I am the LORD.

In order to start his salvation history, God sacrifices Pharaoh and part of his people. Pharaoh and the Egyptians acquire their value and historical meaning as instruments, steering the historical process towards a goal that they do not support, and from which they gain no benefit.

I think these Biblical examples will suffice to show how an instrumental evaluation of men is interwoven in Christian historical thinking. If we wish to see how this trait can come alive when a serious modern Christian tries to apply a Biblical view to our own times it is instructive to study Herbert Butterfield's religious interpretation of the two world wars.[9] He sees these wars as acts of Providence. God uses England to judge Germany, as God used the Philistines to judge his own people. But what about the enormous numbers of starving and maimed children all over Europe. Are they the tools Providence must use to be able to lead history in the right direction?

Anyone who says yes is embracing a metaphysical pattern of history which seems to me both immoral and dangerous. The best moral corrective, as I see it, is Kant's second formulation of the categorical imperative: always treat mankind as ends, never merely as means. If Providence is characterized by goodness, I think it adheres to this rule.

Let me now repeat the ethical arguments. Theories that involve metaphysical patterns of history are often criticized for lending support to the suppression of human beings, both individually and as groups. I have argued that they can indeed have such an effect if they contain a principle that I have called the instrumental evaluation of men. Metaphysical patterns that support this principle should therefore be avoided. I then went on to show that this criterion involves the rejection of a certain part of the traditional Christian pattern of history.

Before ending this part of my argument I wish to make a few brief comments on other arguments adduced against certain metaphysical patterns of history, or more specifically against tendencies to reductionism. In describing the first defining characteristic of metaphysical patterns of history, I indicated what is here meant by reductionism, distinguishing between patterns that contain this tendency and those that do not. To enter upon any conclusive argumentation in this context would take us too far afield, and I must simply trust you will agree with me that the non-reductionist approach is to be preferred. This point is not, in the theological perspective, as important as the former one. There is, however, in the Christian reflection of history, a tendency to observe only the belief-related factors – what men believe and wear in their hearts. Social structures, for instance, and class struggles are not regarded as decisive in history. Let it suffice to say that these tendencies lead us in a wrong direction when developed into a reductionist approach to historical explanation.

Let me sum up my argument at this point. I said that it would be of great importance if we could find a good metaphysical pattern of history. I have now considered some standard arguments directed against the theories that form metaphysical patterns of history.

This discussion has produced two kinds of result.

The first is a set of criteria which a "good" metaphysical pattern must satisfy. Let us repeat these minimum criteria. The first was a general criterion to the effect that the pattern must be compatible with historical facts, and capable of lending a Gestalt to more than narrow sections of the historical process. The remaining criteria can be summed up easily enough if we recall the distinction made previously between "hard" och "soft" metaphysical patterns of history. It will have emerged by now that all the damaging arguments are directed against hard metaphysical patterns. If we are looking for a good metaphysical pattern of history, we must look for a soft one. I am afraid that Popper's arguments against historicism have been read as destroying all metaphysics of history. I hope that the terminology I have used here makes it clear that this is a mistake. Most of his arguments are conclusive only against a "hard" metaphysics of history.

The second kind of result is the theological results. We have seen that many Christian theories of history must be regarded as building-stones for bad metaphysical patterns of history.

My first example was a Gestalt which Cullman claims to be Biblical. I hope that you can see by now that my subsequent examples are related to this Gestalt. There are Christian ideas of history which are built on a doubtful Gestalt and, when taken together, make up a hard metaphysical pattern of history. From the general theological position that I described in my introduction, this Christian pattern of history must be rejected. It is sometimes referred to under the term "salvation history", but this term is used in many senses.

I shall now begin to discuss whether the Christian tradition also contains ideas that can contribute to a metaphysical pattern of history which fulfils our criteria. I am not pretending, as does Reinhold Niebuhr, to describe any sort of "Biblical conception of history". Although sympathizing with Niebuhr's theology of history, I believe it utterly impossible to make any synthesis of the different views of history contained in the Bible. The great difference between Niebuhr's Biblical conception of history and Cullmann's is instructive in this respect. My aim is much more modest than Niebuhr's. I wish, simply, to reflect upon the various Christian traditions that have emerged from the Biblical sources, and try to establish, with the help of my criteria, whether we can find in them some building-stones for a good metaphysical pattern of history.

A good starting-point will be to consider such theological ideas as may help us to form a Gestalt of the historical process. The basis here is a doctrine which we must assume to be inseparable from Christian theology. We can call it the idea of "God's involvement in history". It claims that God is in some way present in the course of events which can be studied historically. In the ordinary course of events, men can meet God. If we take away this idea, nothing whatsoever is left of the Old Testament theologies. The entire New Testament, too, is built on the conviction of men being addressed by God in a series of historical events. In this general form, no theologian has denied the doctrine. Bultmann clearly denies the possibility of an objective pattern of history like Cullmann's, and is critical regarding the historical truth of the New Testament. He remarks, however, that every moment in our temporal process can be an eschatological moment – which is the same as saying that God is present and can be encountered in our historical reality. Now this claim of God's involvement in history is a very far-reaching metaphysical idea, and it is not easy to make it clear without coming into conflict with certain basic principles of our present world-view. We need to reflect very carefully on this basis of a Christian pattern of history. What I can offer constitutes little more than a few introductory remarks.

The Christian God is thought of as existing independently of the universe.

God is not material, and can exist without the material world. This is generally, and I think inescapably, included in our concept of God. Such a being cannot be conceived of as bound by our everyday concept of time, which is linked to processes in the material world. It is ridiculous to imagine an immaterial being having a spiritual watch. The idea of time underlying a scheme like Cullmann's often involves a trivial philosophical confusion. Time cannot be analysed as a stream flowing endlessly forward. This becomes apparent if we enquire as to the speed of this temporal stream. We will then require a concept of time with the help of which we can measure or estimate the development of time – a hypertime. And if this time is to be analysed in the same way, we obtain an infinite regression.

The problems involved in the concept of time have been clear to Christian thinking long before the analyses of modern philosophy, and the complications of the linear concept of time in modern physics. It is common to refer at this point to St. Augustine, but let us take another example from the early Church. One of the Cappadocian fathers, Gregory of Nazianzus, argues in his third theological oration, against the Arian idea that there was a time when the Son did not exist. His argument is that temporal concepts are not applicable to God. We cannot, therefore, meaningfully ask when the Son came into being. He is, as Gregory says, "above all 'When'"[10]

Returning now to the involvement of God in history, this must mean an involvement in the temporal process of something transcending time. Since, according to a generally accepted Christian idea, God is present everywhere, it also means an involvement of something transcending our concept of space. This is often stated in theology. Having said so much, however, the real problem remains. How can we get any meaning into the expression "transcending time and space"?

Can we point to any analogy, or to any other use of the verb "transcend" which is similar to the present one? And how are we to explain the relationship between this transcendent element and the entities studied by the scientists and historians? These questions are overly neglected in theology, and all talk of God-involvement thus easily becomes void of content as soon as it leaves the naive level. A theologian who has something important to say here is the German, Karl Heim, whose theories I believe to be unduly neglected. Let me give a fairly free summary of a part of Heim's theory in answer to our questions.[11]

A key concept in Heim's theory is the "system of dimension". An example of a system including only one dimension is an infinite line. Space as we know it is a system of three dimensions, and in modern science a four-dimensional system is often used. When we add a new dimension to a system of dimensions, a new possibility is opened up which did not exist in the more limited system. We can imagine a system in which the entities are ordered in a single dimension, namely time. It is then true of two entities, A and B, that either there is a time difference between them, or they are identical. But if we add a single spatial dimension, a new possibility opens up: A and B can be contemporary but not identical.

It is now possible to imagine our reality being described with the help of more dimensions than those we use in everyday life and in science. To say that there exists a transcendent God can mean, against this background, first the addition of a new dimension to our normal system of dimensions, and second that we must imagine God as existing in this richer system of dimensions. We can have no clear idea of this form of existence. It is as difficult as it would be for a flat being, living in a space with the dimensions only of length and breadth, to conceive of a body in three-dimensional space. We can, however, imagine without difficulty that there may be a kind of existence in a system of more dimensions. It is further true, as I have already said, that new possibilities are opened up if we add a new dimension. It can therefore be true that God has such properties as omnipresence, which are quite impossible for a being living in the system of dimensions with which we are acquainted.

The basic claim in a Christian view of history can now be made somewhat more distinct. It implies that there is a further dimension in which every historical event can be seen – a dimension beyond those we are familiar with in our everyday lives or reckon with in science. This further dimension cannot be visualized. Sometimes, however, we experience that we are meeting a reality in this new dimension – a reality of a personal kind. This is an experience of God's involvement in history. We can interpret its meaning with the help of analogies and metaphors, and form an idea of God. When the new dimension becomes apparent in a striking way in some ordinary course of events, we speak of a revelation in history. God-experiences in history are to be distinguished from another kind of experiences which are also common in Christianity, as they are in other religions. These we can call mystical experiences. Here men meet God not as a new dimension to historical events, but as a new dimension in their inner life. I think we can say that the Christian tradition is made up of God-encounters of both kinds. But by comparison with, say, Indian religion, a greater stress is laid on the historical encounter. The theology of history is therefore important in Christian theology.

We have now taken the first step in forming a Christian pattern of history. This step involves seeing the whole historical process as not only created by God, but also open to God. God is involved in everything that happens, down to the falling of sparrows. He is the God of Neanderthal Man and of Cro-Magnon Man, and he is no less present in the history of the Inca people than in that of the Israelites.

The special importance of the Israelite people lies in their interpretations of God-encounters in their history, interpretations making up, together, an image of God which is subsequently clarified and made definite through the Christ-event. I shall be returning to this point later on.

The next Gestalt-forming point in a Christian view of history can be termed the "dramatic perspective". Christian theologians, in their interpretation of the work of Christ, have always seen an element of struggle. God fights in Christ against the forces of evil. The Swedish theologian Gustaf Aulén has clearly pointed out how central this idea is in early Christology. He further argues that the entire work of God in his Creation must be seen as a dramatic fight against evil.[12] If we are to say that God is totally good and loving, then I think this idea is a necessary complement to what has been said about the presence of God. It follows that there will always be taking place, in history, a fight between good and evil forces. The presence of God in history is a presence on the side of the good in this battle. Therefore, the involvement of God cannot mean that he is the author of everything that happens. The providence of God, seen from the human point of view, can mean that every historical situation contains the possibility of a good development, an opening to a transcendent goodness. A meaningful human life in history is a life in which a human being realizes some of these good possibilities. In religious terms, the image of God is thereby being established. This is something that can happen in all ages and cultures.

Now it is possible to point out, in the Christian tradition, a serious threat to the power-perspective. A Christian view of God's revelation suggests the importance of observing the kind of reality in which that revelation is found. The history, in other words, of a suppressed people, of poor men, of daily life in the villages, of human beings who give of their own for their fellow-men. This perspective of history is a perspective from below.

You are all, I imagine, familiar with thoughts like these, but it is astonishing how very little they have meant in Christian historical thinking. Even Church history is traditionally seen in the power-perspective. The idea of history from below, which is so firmly connected with a Christian view of God's revelation in history, has become more established among the historians of our own day. I think we are bound to give the credit for this to a large extent to Marxism. Inspired by Marxist thinking, many historians have now tried to write a history of the suppressed. And various Marxist ideas have probably helped to create a climate in which there is a growing interest in social history. There is no doubt that historical materialism is in clear contradiction to certain basic Christian doctrines. But in stressing a perspective from below, Marxism may be preserving a Christian idea that many Christians have forgotten.

I mentioned earlier the change in historical prespective that has emerged in the feminist movement. This is a change in the same direction. Observing the roles of women in different historical processes, we often find ourselves getting a perspective from below and are brought straight into social history. I believe that something important can happen in this field, on two conditions. The first is that feminist studies should be performed in a scholarly manner, which, unfortunately, is far from always the case. The second is that we should not find ourselves left simply with a feminization of the power-perspective. With Bloody Mary occupying centre stage, and so on.

I have now mentioned three Christian ideas that can help us to form a

Gestalt in history. These were the idea of God-involvement in history, the dramatic view, including the idea of a victory in Christ, and the perspective from below. From the viewpoint of the secularized historian, these ideas are extremely pretentious, and make great metaphysical claims. Quoting Karl Heim, I have indicated a way in which these claims can be rendered comprehensible, and defensible. For those who may be expecting a detailed picture of historical development, these three sets of Christian ideas which I have considered probably say too little. The question of whether historical development is linear or circular, or as Toynbee claims, both, has been left open. What I have said offers no forecast of the future course of history, is of no help in the periodization of history. If these problems can be solved at all, they must be solved by historical research. This research also contains an element of Gestaltformation, which will meet a religious Gestalt. Christianity, in the view put forward, does not offer a ready-made outline of the historical process like an aerial photograph taken by an angel – but provides the historian with frameworks, contours and guidelines. It also puts certain limits to the historian's Gestalt-formation.

I have emphasized that Gestalt-formation of the kind involved here is firmly connected with value factors. This is obviously true of the Gestalt-forming factors that I have been discussing here. Our next step must be to make explicit the value-scale interwoven with these theoretical aspects.

It is a well-known phenomenon in religions that the religious man can turn his attention from this world and from profane history in order to concentrate on God and heavenly things. In Christianity, however, this tendency is balanced by the doctrine of God's involvement in history. It is therefore possible that – as frequently remarked – the Judeo-Christian religion has promoted an interest in history. We must be careful, however, to avoid any such vast simplification as to draw, say, a straight line from St. Augustine's theology of history to modern historical research. I do, on the other hand, think it obvious that the aspects of the theology of history that I discussed above can provide, today, a basis for ascribing a high value to historical knowledge. Given the doctrine of God's universal involvement in history, all kinds of historical facts acquire religious significance. This high valuation of history and stimulation of historical interest is the first value-element that must be underlined in a Christian pattern of history.

The next value-element is considerably more complicated. It relates to the ethical building-stones which make up the dramatic perspective. I do not intend to discuss this here in any detail. Let me, simply, remind you of one of the key concepts involved, namely that of "true" human nature. The meaning of "true" humanity can be seen in Christ. The dominating trait is an agapistic attitude. A true human life is one characterized by unselfish love, flowing freely from the centre of our personality. This is what God, who is agape, is fighting to establish – the image of God in the world. An ethical tendency of this kind also opens up the possibility of our learning from history. Historical knowledge can help us to identify the threats that exist to true humanity, and to be on the side of God in the drama. But if it is to afford us this help, the historical reality must be seen to a certain extent from below. We can notice here how the different Gestalt-forming traits are connected.

One of the functions of metaphysical patterns of history, by our definition, is to support and express a basic emotional experience of life. How, then, can we describe the basic experience connected with the Christian ideas of history that I have dealt with? I think that there is no better word than "hope". But if our argument so far is correct, Christian hope cannot reasonably be based on expectations of a happy historical future. Nor, even, on a happy historical end. We do not, however, need any very detailed theory as to the course of history in order to obtain an anchorage for hope. If the metaphysical pattern of history is built up from the foundation I described previously, then there is a two-fold basis for hope. The first is that every new situation contains the possibility of a good development – the possibility of realizing a loving relationship, among men or between God and man. This is what the presence of God implies. The second basis is our belief in the victory of love as seen in Christ. This, however, is a victory which transcends history. I argued , that it cannot reasonably be made the basis of any prophecy. History is waiting to be fulfilled not at the end of history, but at the end of every human life.

The first point in my definition of a metaphysical pattern of history was a function that I called the gradation of types of explanatory factors. My motive for including this characteristic in my definition was to avoid incorporating in this class of theories those *Weltanschauungen* which are loosely related to historical studies. This characteristic links metaphysical patterns to concrete attempts to explain a given historical development. The group of theological ideas on which I have now been concentrating also have a role to play in this respect, and they undoubtedly fulfil the requirements of a metaphysical pattern of history.

According to the Christian ideas to which I have drawn attention, God is at work in history when men adopt a certain ethical attitude. This implies that human thoughts and responsible value-judgments are of basic importance in history. They must therefore be given priority in our explanation of an historical process. Given this perspective, it is absolutely impossible to explain them in terms of, say, forces in the material world. We have here an obvious contradiction with historical materialism. A Christian and a Marxist pattern of history, as backgrounds to historical research, will thus produce different results with regard to historical explanations. Christian historians, however, have often stressed the ideological factors to the point of reductionism. It is important to see that the assignment of priority to one type of factor does not entail the exclusion of others. There is no ground, in the Christian pattern we have dealt with, for disregarding the material basis of men's behaviour or the psychological forces that are at work. And in this respect other metaphysical patterns of history can constitute valuable correctives to a Christian view.

Before leaving this point, I must turn my attention to a set of questions that I have so far avoided. Is it not the case, according to any Christian view, that certain events require a special religious explanation? Does not God operate, in certain cases, as a causal factor in the empirical world? Or, to put it another way, must we not reckon with miracles in the course of history? These questions raise a whole complex of theological problems, which I will try here to avoid. In the present context, I think it will suffice to refer to the theory of dimensions that I discussed last time. Scholarly research in the field of history is a work performed in our everyday dimensions. It is in this perspective that we try to understand what has happened. And we have succeeded in formulating certain rules for the discovery and explanation of past actions. But if we introduce the direct involvement of God among our causal factors, we shall be transcending the system of dimensions in which historical work is performed. Such a step will lead either to a system of explanation and understanding in which entirely different rules must hold, or else to our trying to retain the normal system of rules and standards while introducing an entity that can only be understood in a more inclusive system of dimensions, in which case our explanation is bound to collapse.

We can now summarize the ideas in Christianity which, taken together, can provide the incitement to a good metaphysical pattern of history. Let me do this by listing some key phrases at each of the three points of my definition.

(1) Priority to ideological or "belief-related" factors in historical explanation, in a non-reductionist way.

(2) God's involvement in history.
    A dramatic view, including the doctrine of a victory in Christ.
    A perspective from below.

(3) A basic attitude of hope (which is not anchored in long-term prophecies).
    Agape – the main characteristic of true humanity.
    The importance of historical knowledge.

Comparing these ideas with the much more explicit historical theories that I have critizised, I think that a theologian is bound to ask one question in particular: "What are we to do in theology with all the historical or historylike texts of the Bible?" Let me first draw attention, briefly, to two schemes of interpretation that will be impossible if we wish to avoid a "bad" metaphysical pattern of history. One interpretation which must definitely be rejected is to take the historical events recorded in the Bible as the contours of a definitive Gestalt, within which we can include the total history of the world. According to our previous arguments, we cannot – without leaving the realm of responsible metaphysics – go further in concrete terms than to maintain the idea of a God-involvement in all history, a dramatic view, and a perspective from below. A second way of interpreting the chain of historical events in the Old

and New Testaments, which our arguments render doubtful but not impossible, is to see Biblical history as a movement towards a fulfilment. In interpreting the Old Testament, von Rad, in his admirable book *Old Testament Theology*,[13] puts fairly strong emphasis on this idea. The fulfilment is the Christ-
event. It can also be claimed that the historical development recorded in the
New Testament points to the ultimate fulfilment, in the Second Coming of
Christ. The greatest problem involved in maintaining a more limited Gestalt
of this kind is that it can so easily become the anchorage for an instrumental
evaluation of men. It can also provide the foundation for an instrumental
evaluation of the Jewish religion. This is not a decisive argument against it,
but it does afford reason to be cautious in its use. I also think that if we look at
other modes of interpreting the historical texts, it will emerge as less important.

Seen from the standpoint which I have defended the main religious interest
of the Bible's historical texts lies in their claim to be reports of God-encounters
in historical events. Many historical texts in the Bible can be seen as
testimonies of men and women who have discovered the God-dimension in
historical events, and who are struggling to explain and interpret their
experiences. Their interpretations differ widely, and it is difficult, I think, to
point to any clear development. A Christian, however, believes that he
possesses, in Christ, a measure that can tell him something of the adequacy of
earlier attempts to understand the God of history. But it is also true that the
revelation in Christ can only be understood with the help of concepts and
thought-processes worked out in earlier attempts to interpret the presence of
God.

The historical texts are not only reports of God-encounters in history. Some
of them can also be seen as paradigms for such encounters. They can thereby
assist people in quite different situations to see God in contemporary history.
The main historical paradigm in the Old Testament, of course, is the Exodus
story, and we can see how freely this has been used in different historical
situations. I believe that many historical texts in the Bible can have the same
function today. They can help us to see the presence of God in victory and in
defeat alike, and they can underline the importance of taking the side of God
in the battle between good and evil.

There is also a third use of historical texts, the one that from the historical
perspective of Christian doctrine is the most important. This is when historical narratives in the Bible are used typologically, and applied to the Christian
Church or to the individual Christian. We all know that the New Testament
writers use Old Testament texts in this way. This approach was subsequently
applied within the Church, and it was systematized by Origen. This is
something we can study in the textbooks under the heading of "The four
senses of Scripture". I do feel, however, that those who have not considered
very closely the development of Christian theology from the Early Church up
to the Schoolmen tend to underestimate the enormous importance of this

typological way of reading the Bible. Of particular interest is the fact that the historical narratives have had the power to illustrate and express very basic experiences in personal religious life in different periods of history and in different cultures. Perhaps this is one of the main reasons why these curious details from world-history should have survived so vigorously in our civilisation. I also think that the historical text will continue to have a great importance of this kind in people's religious lives. We can explain this, as Bultmann has done, with the help of existentialist philosophy, but it is not, of course, necessary to take this particular philosophical road.

I have spoken of historical texts. It may, however, be worth mentioning at this point that some of these texts are of cultic origin, and have therefore been connected from the beginning with religious experiences relating to the individual.

Our awareness of the cultic origins of certain historical narratives is one of the results of historical research in the field of the Old Testament. During the past 50 years, historical Biblical research has given us a quite new picture of the development of Old and New Testament religion. I do not intend to consider the well-known problems with which this knowledge has presented theology. Let me only remark that a critical historical evaluation of the Biblical texts is perfectly compatible with their theological function of building up a metaphysical pattern of history, provided this pattern has the characteristic traits that I have suggested, and the theological function of the texts is regarded in the way I have indicated.

I will now move on to my closing section. In this, I will deal briefly with the question whether an appeal to history can be used as an argument for Christianity. The most common use of apologetic arguments from history is not as proofs for the truth of Christianity. They are generally used in combination with other arguments, and are seen as lending additional support to a Christian view of life. Our question will therefore be whether it is possible to lend any support to Christianity by appealing to history.

Against this background, it is easy to see that certain types of argument – and types of argument that are frequently used – are necessarily untenable. Let me mention two examples. Many theologians have tried to show that the study of certain events – such as the Resurrection of Christ – by means of ordinary historical methods forces us to introduce God as an explanatory factor. I have specifically studied such arguments in the theological debate prior to Hume's famous essay on miracles, and I have shown where the logical mistake lies.[14] I shall not repeat that argument here. It will suffice to refer what I have said earlier on concerning the fallacious mixture of systems of dimension in these arguments. This is a road definitely closed to any modern apologist. Another example of an impossible road from history to Christian belief is to point to a system of rewards and punishments in the course of history, and then claim that this scheme indicates the existence of a Divine Providence. Disregarding the numerous other problems here involved, we have seen that a God whose existence could be made probable in this way must on frequent occasions be a God who embraces an instrumental evaluation of men, and is thereby not a Christian God.

In my opinion, there is only one way in which we can lend support to Christian belief by appealing to history. This is if we find, in our search for a metaphysical pattern of history, that a Christian pattern stands out as adequate. I have tried to show in my former arguments first that the search for a metaphysical pattern of history is a meaningful and important intellectual task, second that a good metaphysical pattern of history must fulfil three criteria, and third that, although many popular Christian patterns must be rejected, the Bible, and Christian tradition, do contain some building-stones suitable for a good metaphysical pattern of history. If we are now to use these results in an argument for Christian belief, one thing remains to be done, namely to discuss whether the good Christian pattern can be shown to be an adequate one. The first step has been taken once we have demonstrated that it fulfils the criteria, but this is not enough. The criteria I have used are minimum requirements. It is perfectly possible that several different metaphysical patterns of history will satisfy these criteria. Among these "good" patterns, one may be experienced as adequate and therefore to be preferred. What, then, is involved in finding a good metaphysical pattern of history adequate? This is a problem we must deal with briefly. First of all we must realize that we do not have before us a given number of indisputable historical facts, which we should try to order by finding a Gestalt. The experiential basis for a metaphysical pattern of history is in no way something fixed. I think that one of the main reasons why different people prefer different metaphysical patterns of history is that they start from different experiences.

To claim that a metaphysical pattern of history is adequate therefore involves stating on what experiences it is based. The pattern is not a conclusion from these experiences, but a way of ordering and interpreting them. To find out whether the interpretation is correct, we have, as I explained in the first part of this essay, to rely in part on an experience analagous to that of seeing a Gestalt.

We can now see how any argument for the adequacy of a Christian pattern of history must be conducted. The most important task is to indicate the experience on which it is based. When someone shares this experiential basis, we have to appeal to and rely on the Gestalt-experience that can emerge when the pattern is presented – an experience well-known even in the formation of general scientific theories. Those who find a Christian pattern adequate thereby have an indication of the credibility of a Christian doctrine.

Let us now deal with certain traits in the experiential basis of a Christian pattern of history. As in all metaphysical patterns of history, the most important aspect, of course, is the historical facts made known to us by empirical research. I am not going to deal with the problems involved in establishing historical facts belonging to our empirical reality. But an important point in metaphysics is what we are to do with all the reports we have from all over the world concerning God-encounters in historical series of events. Are they based on experiences of a further dimension in our reality, or are they mere illusions and superstition? This will have a decisive bearing on our choice of a metaphysical pattern of history. A materialistic pattern involves seeing them as illusions. Many of us, however, have ourselves experienced meeting God in the ordinary course of events. It will then be very difficult for us to see all these experiences as illusions. If we try to take them as being, sometimes, experiences of reality, then we have here an anchorage for a Christian pattern of history. This pattern interprets such God-experiences, and relates them to the general course of history. However, we must be more specific at this point. According to the Christian pattern, these experiences are most clear in series of events in which men give of their own, and sacrifice themselves for others. If this corresponds to our own experience, then we have a further factor that reinforces a Christian pattern. Another experience which many people in our generation have had, and which is given interpretation in the Christian dramatic perspective, can be called the experience of the strength of evil. Evil appears to be so firmly rooted in our nature, and in our various societies, that we cannot hope to rid ourselves of it by education, or by organization, or by some mysterious evolutionary process. Reinhold Niebuhr has explained how this experience of the weight of evil finds its interpretation in a Christian view of history, and I believe him to be entirely right in this.[15] But there is also another experience, balancing the weight of evil. That is the experience of the strength of love. A Christian pattern will include the strength of love in its Gestalt of historical development by assigning a central position to the cross of Christ, seen as a victory. Other experiences and value-judgments incorporated in a Christian pattern relate to the importance of personal decisions for the course of world events, and the great weight assigned to the lives of the poor and the oppressed in world history.

I do not believe that the experiences to which I have now briefly drawn attention exist independently of Christian theology, and that a Christian pattern of history can simply refer to them. There is a complicated interplay between the pattern and what is experienced. Sometimes the pattern will open up possibilities for us to discern new aspects of reality. But what I am claiming, above all, is that many people have the capacity to share the experiential basis of a Christian pattern of history, and therefore find this pattern helpful and adequate for their orientation in reality. In this way, the working out and testing of a Christian pattern of history can lend support to Christian belief. It is therefore extremely important, from the Christian point of view, that we should rid ourselves of those patterns which do not fulfil the minimum criteria for a good pattern of history. If presented as the only Christian alternative, they lend actual support to a non-Christian metaphysic of history. It must also be observed that I have not presented a complete "good Christian pattern of history" – only some building-stones and guidelines. To complete the picture will require both historical knowledge and theological imagination. The goal must be to do justice to the moral and religious life, without negating the knowledge that is based on science, or the results of scholarly research. And with this I have formulated, once again, the theological programme outlined in the introduction to this book.

NOTES

[1] K R Popper, *The Poverty of Historicism*, 2nd ed London 1960, p 3. Popper's other great and well-known work in this field is *The Open Society and its Enemies*. London 1945.

[2] Spengler's book was translated into English in 1926 entiteled *The Decline of the West*.

[3] There is an useful abridgement of Toynbee's *A Study of History* by D C Somervell, Oxford 1946 and 1957. See to this point for instance Chapter XXI in Somervell's first volume.

[4] G H von Wright, *Tanke och förkunnelse*, Helsingfors 1955.

[5] See for instance Erik H Erikson, *Young Man Luther, A Study in Psychoanalysis and History*, New York 1958.

[6] E Nagel, "Some Issues in the Logic of Historical Analysis", in *Theories of History* ed by Patrick Gardiner, New York 1959, pp 382 ff.

[7] Reprinted many times, see for instance *Werke 12*, 1980.

[8] R Bultmann, "Heilsgeschichte und Geschichte. Über O Cullmanns, Christus und die Zeit", *ThLZ* 1948, Sp 659ff.

[9] See for instance Herbert Butterfield, *Christianity and History*, London 1949. The example referred to in the text is to be found on p 52.

[10] *A Select Library of Nicene and Post-Nicene Fathers of the Christian Church*, 2nd Series. Ed by P Schaff & H Wace, Vol VII, Ann Arbor 1974, p 301.

[11] See further Ingemar Holmstrand, *Karl Heim on Philosophy, Science and the Transcendence of God*, Uppsala 1980.

[12] Auléns most well-known book is perhaps *Christus Victor*, English translation 1931.

[13] The book was published in German 1957–60. English translation 1962–65.

[14] See my book *Butler and Hume on Religion, A Comparative Analysis*, Stockholm 1966, Chapt V.

[15] See for instance Reinhold Niebuhr, *Faith and History*, 1949.

Index of names

Althaus, P   25 f
Aquinas   26
Aristotle   55
Augustine   47, 52, 61
Aulén, G   63, 71
Austin, I L   19, 28
Barr, J   40, 45
Barth, K   19, 27, 28
Bausani, A   13
Berkeley, G   24, 29
Bochenski, J   26, 27
Boyle, Robert   10
Browne, P   24, 29
Brunner, E   25
Bultmann, R   53, 60, 71
Butler, J   32, 44 f, 71
Butterfield, H   58, 71
Carnap   26
Chardin, T de   37
Comenius, A   13
Confucius   55
Couterat, L   13
Cullman, O   47, 53 ff, 71
Decartes, R   13

Derham, W   10
Erigena, Johannes Scotus   13
Erikson, E   71
Frankena, W K   44
Frängsmyr, T   13
Gardiner, P   71
Gregory Nanzianzus   61
Hanson, R P C   44, 45
Hanson, A T   44, 45
Hegel, Fr   48, 50
Heim, K   61, 64
Hick, J   21
Holmstrand, I   71
Hospers, J   32, 44
Hume, David   10, 68, 71
Jeffner, A   28 f, 44, 71
Johnson, P   37, 45
Küng, H   41
Leau, L   13
Leibniz, G W von   14 ff
Lullus, R   13
Luther, M   48, 50
Mackei, J L   45
Nagel, E   48, 71

Niebuhr, R   70, 71
Nietzsche, Fr   52
Nineham, D   40
Nygren, A   45
Palgarno, G   13
Palmer, H   24
Pannenberg, W   47, 56
Popper, K R   47 f, 55 f, 57, 71
Price, H H   45
Quick, O   44
Rad, G von   67
Ramsey, I   25
Ross, D   44
Russell, B   16 f
Schaff, P   71
Schweitzer, A   56
Spengler, O   47, 49, 71
Svedenborg, E   13
Tillich, P   37
Toynbee   47, 49, 64, 71
Weber, O   45
Wilkins, J   9 ff
Wittgenstein, L   16 f
Wright, G H von   47, 71